T · H · E

# ROLE
## OF
# WOMEN
## IN
# MINISTRY
# TODAY

# Other Books by H. Wayne House

Schooling Choices
Civilization in Crisis
Dominion Theology: Blessing or Curse?
Restoring the Constitution
Divorce and Remarriage: Four Christian Views
Chronological and Background Charts of the New
Testament

# T · H · E
# ROLE
## OF
# WOMEN
## IN
# MINISTRY
# TODAY

## H. WAYNE HOUSE

Published in Nashville, Tennessee, by Thomas Nelson, Inc. and distributed in Canada by Lawson Falle, Ltd., Cambridge, Ontario.

Unless stated otherwise, translations, or paraphrases of Scripture in this
book are the author's.

**Library of Congress Cataloging-in-Publication Data**

House, H. Wayne
    The role of women in ministry today / H. Wayne House
    Includes bibliographical references.
    ISBN 0-8407-3044-6
    1. Ordination of women—Controversial literature.   2. Women in
church work.   3. Women in Christianity.   4. Evangelicalism
BV676.H675   1990                                               89-49746
262' 1'082—dc20                                                     CIP

Printed in the United States of America
1 2 3 4 5 6 7—95 94 93 92 91 90

*To Larry and Mary Catherine White, friends who have traveled with me through the long birthing of this book.*

# Contents

# Acknowledgments

I wish to thank Richard Greene, a graduate assistant to me at Dallas Seminary for his help on 1 Corinthians 14:34–35. Also, Ken Durham provided invaluable assistance to me during the writing process.

Special thanks are due to Dr. Everett Ferguson of Abilene Christian University who supervised my master's research on women in the ante-Nicaean church, and to Dr. Armin Moellering of Concordia Seminary, St. Louis, who supervised my doctoral research in feminist hermeneutics in Paul's writings on women.

I appreciate the permission given by *Bibliotheca Sacra*, journal of Dallas Theological Seminary, to include materials printed in that journal.

Lastly, I wish to say thanks to many faculty and students at Dallas Seminary for their interaction with much of the argumentation in this book and their biblical view on men and women in the face of a strong cultural wind to the contrary.

# Introduction

In this day of social upheaval, many traditional views held by the Christian church are being questioned. Not the least important of these is the issue of women in ministry. During the past several decades, the feminist movement has had significant impact on the church; this impact is such that the issues feminist scholarship has raised simply cannot be ignored or avoided.

Churches, denominations, and even Christian organizations have been split asunder over the issue of ordaining women for pulpit ministry. Of equal concern, well-meaning and dedicated Christian women who desire to serve the Lord are confused and confounded by contradictory arguments about the proper role of women in the church.

Until recent years, the role of women in the church had generally been considered a settled matter. Except for a few outbreaks of unconventional theology (such as in Montanism, Gnosticism, and movements given to the pursuit of ecstatic experiences), Christian tradition and practice has held that women are not to occupy positions of leadership in the church, most notably the more prominent and visible positions of pastor, teacher (specifically, over men), and elder.

Although barring women from these positions, the church has held that many other places of service are available to women. The emphasis during much of church history, however, was on leadership restrictions imposed on women rather than on the various ways in which women could serve in the church. Because the church continues to focus on these restrictions, the book by necessity must concern itself primarily with the biblical passages which deal with restrictions and qualifications for church leadership. In the closing chapter, however, the author will also touch on some of the roles for ministry which are biblically open to women and which are, in fact, often better suited to godly women than to godly men.

In light of the current controversy surrounding the issue of women in ministry, Christian leaders would be irresponsible not to explore the Word of God objectively to see if women have indeed been arbitrarily disqualified from functions in the church which are biblically open to them. We must approach the Scriptures with an openness that will allow us to recognize and freely acknowledge the great value of godly women in biblical ministry. This openness, however, must not be at the expense of any teaching of Scripture that sets limits on women's roles of service.

Sincere Christians stand on both sides of this issue. Some believe women may occupy any and all positions in the church, even those historically reserved for men. Others believe that just as God reserved certain areas of Old Testament worship and service for the tribe of Levi, He has reserved certain areas of ministry in the New Testament Church for those who meet other predetermined qualifications—including in some cases a qualification of gender. We must respect both views and approach the matter of women's role in ministry with a gentle and accommodating spirit. At the same time, our ultimate authority in resolving the issue must be God's will as revealed in His Word.

## FOUR PURPOSES

This book will seek to accomplish four purposes. **First,** the author will examine the arguments of those contemporary scholars who believe Paul the apostle's teachings permitted and even encouraged women to occupy key teaching and leadership roles in the church. **Second,** the author will outline his understanding of the New Testament's teaching on women in ministry. **Third,** the author will present the ministry role of women in the ante-Nicaean church (the church preceding the Council of Nicaea), information which provides verification and examples of the role of women in the first three centuries of the church. **Fourth,** the author will suggest ways in which women may serve biblically and effectively in the work of the church.

Within each of these broader divisions, essential passages of Scripture, philosophical and historical developments, and contemporary arguments will be examined. In every work that seeks to address essential Christian issues, the author must make a choice concerning how much energy he will spend defining and answering erroneous thought, and how much energy he will devote to tracing God's revelation in Scripture and the historical response of the church to that revelation. Because the author of this book desires to address essential concepts rather than discredit individuals, the great majority of the book's content will focus on knowing and understanding God's Word on the matter of women in ministry. If one or more lines of argumentation that militate against a biblical view of women in ministry are overlooked or ignored, it is most likely that the particular point of view disavows the Bible as an infallible foundation of authority. Without an objective basis of truth and authority, argumentation is useless.

The book rests on several assumptions made without further qualification. The first is that the Bible is inspired; that is, it is literally and entirely "God-breathed." The second is that the Bible is God's infallible, inerrant, inscripturated revelation to man, entirely true and without error in the original manuscripts. The third is that the Bible is an authoritative, uncompromised guide to Christian conviction as well as Christian behavior today. And the fourth is that a consistent, historical/grammatical method of interpretation must be applied to the Scriptures in order to correctly assess which portions of it are culturally conditioned and which portions transcend matters of culture, custom, and historical setting.

The greatest need for addressing the issue of the role of women in ministry today is that it touches the very heart of leadership, ministry, order, and authority in the church of Jesus Christ. Moreover, because no philosophy is static, our entire belief system can be affected by the conclusions we draw—particularly because this issue calls into question the believability and applicability of portions of God's Word.

Thus the issue of women in ministry, which has been forced upon us largely by the feminist movement in secular society, cannot and should not be ignored. It must be addressed not only to provide a reasonable answer for those who would contest God's will as revealed in His Word, but also to provide a source of confidence and reassurance for believers who sincerely seek biblical answers, regardless of how those answers may or may not conform to modern culture.

Only with all this in view can we move sensitively and confidently forward, letting our conclusions shape our convictions, rather than vice versa.

T · H · E

# ROLE
### OF
# WOMEN
### IN
# MINISTRY
# TODAY

## CHAPTER ONE

# Feminism in the Church

## CONTEMPORARY EVANGELICAL PERSPECTIVES ON THE ROLE OF WOMEN

First Community Church is in turmoil. Michael and Jane Gregory are one of five founding couples of the church, and have believed since the church began three years ago they should have an equal part in its ministry. Recently Jane has expressed an interest in becoming a member of the pastoral staff and taking every fourth Sunday morning sermon in order to show the community that their church is on the cutting edge of relevant ministry.

Michael, who is a co-pastor of the 150-member church, is in favor of the move. Several of the elders, however, are opposed to it on what they call "biblical grounds." Several women in the church have said they will leave the church if it "promotes sexism" by barring Jane from the pulpit. A few members have presented to the elders a plan for making Jane a member of the church staff, but limiting her to counseling women and teaching women's Bible studies. What would you do?

Evangelicals today offer three primary perspectives on how women may function in the local church and Christian ministries. The first may be called the equalitarian or egalitarian view. This position holds that since men and women equally share the image of God and thus are equal in essence, no functional distinctions should be made between men and women. All Christians should be able to exercise any gift or ability they possess in identical contexts. Those who hold this view would be in favor of making Jane an entirely co-equal member of the pastoral staff, with all the rights and privileges enjoyed by male members of the staff—including pulpit ministry.

The second view holds that women should be restricted from most roles in the church, including pastor, elder, and member of the pastoral staff and Christian education and other church boards. In para-church organizations, too, women should be limited to lesser roles. Proponents of this view would not consider allowing Jane any type of position on the church staff, except perhaps as a church secretary or receptionist.

A third position holds that women should have virtual freedom of service in the New Testament church except as an elder or teacher who reproves, rebukes, instructs, and corrects in righteousness the mixed congregation directly from the Word of God. Under this model a woman may teach and have authority over women in the church, hold a paid position in the church as long as she does not have direct authority over men as an elder, and participate in team-taught Bible studies with men present. Proponents of this view believe that church and para-church organizations may find positions of leadership for women as long as the job descriptions do not violate the spiritual authority of an elder. Christians holding this view would base their decision concerning Jane on two factors: her spiritual qualifications for paid ministry, and the biblical injunctions concerning what women should and should not do in ministry.

Perhaps you already have strong feelings about one or more of these views. Or maybe you have not had the opportunity to formulate an opinion at all. Regardless of where you stand, your final decision should be an informed one, not the product of peer pressure or popular cultural opinion. Our first task is to gain an overview of modern feminism, including its evangelical forms and its basic presuppositions about the whole issue of women's role in the church.

## FEMINISM AND THE BIBLE

Two major problems exist in the thought of some current evangelical feminists. The first is a low view of biblical inspiration; the second is an improper method of biblical interpretation. Because our beliefs about inspiration and interpretation are so important in the process of finding a biblical position on any issue, we need to examine these problems more closely.

### What View of Scripture?

Many evangelical feminists openly claim that the Bible contains errors concerning the role of women in ministry. Clark Pinnock, writing about inerrancy, claims that so-called "moderate" evangelicals (those who advocate limited or non-existent inerrancy) tend to handle the Bible the same way liberals do. He points out that one such author, Paul Jewett, in his book *Man as Male and Female*, even accuses Paul of a sub-Christian view on women in passages he can't harmonize with Galatians 3:28. Pinnock says if it is true the human authors of Scripture could commit such errors, then God does not always speak in Scripture—and therefore the reader must determine when God speaks and when He does not. Pinnock concludes, "In principle this seems to be a liberal, not firmly evangelical, theological methodology, and therefore is a disturbing doctrinal development."[1] Harold Lindsell adds, "At stake here is not the matter of women's liberation. What is the issue for the evangelical is the fact that some of the most ardent advocates of egalitarianism [identical roles for both sexes] in marriage over against hierarchy reach their conclusion by directly and deliberately denying that the Bible is the infallible rule of faith and practice."[2]

Much like Jewett, Virginia Mollenkott declares that Paul contradicted himself in his teaching on women.[3] Interestingly, while she claims that Paul misinterpreted Genesis 2, she does hesitate to call Paul's position an error in Scripture. She claims instead that Paul was thinking through his conflicts aloud. In short, Mollenkott believes Paul interpreted Genesis 2 the way he did because of his social conditioning.

Understanding Scripture in this way opens a virtual Pandora's box in regard to biblical interpretation. In application, this view means that anytime someone disagrees with Scripture, the passage in question may be written off because of the writer's cultural conditioning or "socialization."

Without straining, we could easily regard the holy wars of Joshua as nothing more than cultural (Mollenkott actually argues that the words "God said" were only an assumption of Joshua and therefore constituted socialization).[4] Likewise, we could consider Paul's views on homosexuality as socially adaptable but not universally binding. This, in fact, is an argument used by Mollenkott and Letha Scanzoni to propose that evangelical opposition to some forms of homosexuality is a result of homophobia in present-day society rather than the teaching of Scripture.[5]

There is little question that this arbitrary and entirely subjective method of biblical interpretation goes far beyond acceptable limits of evangelical theology. If areas of disagreement can be eliminated merely by an appeal to socialization, then interpretation literally has no controls, and the concepts of "limited revelation" or "degrees of inspiration" cannot be avoided.

Are we to ignore Paul's arguments that sin came from one man simply because we prefer a model of interpretation formulated by contemporary, atheistic anthropology over traditional interpretation? Likewise, should we refuse to believe in sin because we imagine that Paul merely borrowed his ideas on original sin from rabbinical theology?

Obviously, most evangelicals would answer these questions with a resounding "No!" Yet when the cases presented by many Christian feminists are distilled to their essence, these hypothetical examples are not much different than feminist arguments concerning other Pauline instruction. In such cases, the real question is whether or not all of the Bible is the authoritative, inerrant Word of God, and whether or not one will be submissive to it.

## What method of interpretation?

To determine the method of interpretation most appropriate to apply to the Scriptures, particularly in regard to the issue of women in ministry, we will address four crucial questions.

### Did Jesus contradict the Old Testament?

The comparison of Scripture with Scripture seems to be the chief method of interpretation for evangelical feminists. Jewett justifies the use of this method by saying that Christ's interpretive method is his model. In Mark 10:3–5 the Pharisees asked Christ if His view of divorce was in harmony with the Mosaic Law. Jesus, Jewett says, compared Scripture with Scripture in His answer. While Jesus acknowledged that Mosaic legislation allowed for divorce, He recognized this allowance did not express the true intent of creation for marriage. Jesus, in citing Genesis 1:27 and 2:24, said that God gave permission for divorce in Deuteronomy 24:1 because the hearts of the people were hard—a cultural conditioning. Divorce was not the perfect will of God.

Jewett applies the same reasoning to his interpretation of Paul's instruction concerning women:

> Such reasoning, we submit, is analogous . . . to that which we have followed in seeking to understand the Pauline statement of sexual hierarchy in the light of the creation ordinance of sexual partnership. To say that a man may write a bill of divorce and put away his wife, or to say that woman by definition is subordinate to the man, is to come short of the revealed intent of the Creator; it is to break the analogy of faith.[6]

Unfortunately for him and those who would apply this method of interpretation, Jewett's reasoning presents two severe problems. Specifically:

(a) Jesus was not contradicting the passage in Deuteronomy 24 when He appealed to the creation narrative. He expressed God's original *intention* in comparison to God's *concession*. The Bible holds that God inspired the Deuteronomic legislation; it was not merely a "socialization" apart from God's direction. In fact, God allowed for divorce to assure women protection they otherwise might not have in a male-dominated society. Moreover:

(b) To assert that Paul must be interpreted against his own writings elsewhere is to assume that he misinterpreted the Old Testament in practically all of his writings on women except for Galatians 3:28. The reason this latter passage, which will be discussed in detail later, becomes so important to feminists is that it is the only real passage in the New Testament letters that might appear to prove their view on women. It is evident on closer examination, however, that no tension at all exists between this text and Paul's other writings on the subject.

### Did Paul contradict himself?

Evangelical feminists claim that Paul was confused about his view of women and was not faithful in drawing proper (or inspired) conclusions based on the teachings of Christ. They also say he misinterpreted the second creation narrative in order to propagate the idea that women are inferior. This remarkable view is apparently what motivates Mollenkott to write, "Each of these Pauline contrasts reinforces the impression that according to his rabbinical training Paul believed in female subordination but that according to his Christian vision he believed that the gospel conferred full equality on all believers."[7]

There is, however, another option. That option is that Paul was in perfect harmony with Jesus' view on the equality and role of women, that he correctly understood the presentation of man and woman in Genesis 1 and 2, and that he correctly applied them to the responsibilities of man and woman in the church as well as in the home. Obviously, this option is at odds with those who prefer to see Paul contradicting himself. Feminists who see a contradiction in Paul, however make several false assumptions that inevitably lead them to the wrong conclusions.

**First,** evangelical feminists assume that equality between persons requires that roles be interchangeable. Since Paul regarded women as equal with men (Gal. 3:28), but did not let them teach or exercise authority over men (1 Tim. 2:12), he was contradictory. But this assumption cannot be supported from experience or from the Scriptures. Parents and children, employers and employees, the President and citizens of the United States all are equal as persons, but they have definite differences in roles. Also, while church members are equal in Christ, some members are called to positions of authority in the local congregation, while others are not (1 Thess. 5:12; Titus 1:5; Heb. 13:17; 1 Pet. 5:1–5).

**Second,** evangelical feminists assume that Paul borrowed his views on female subordination from Jewish writings rather than from the Old Testament, and that when he did go to the Old Testament he interpreted it in a rabbinical fashion, which caused him to draw wrong conclusions. But the idea that Paul was referring to rabbinic traditions rather than the Old Testament when he used "law" in 1 Corinthians 14:33b–35 (as Mollenkott for one has suggested) is nothing more than unfounded guesswork. Rabbinic influence on the New Testament writers is questionable: most of the rabbinic writings we have were written centuries after the New Testament, and many probably represent individual ideas rather than a generally held opinion or school of thought. Even if such writings *were* influential, a correct understanding of inspiration would argue that the apostle Paul would not have used them wrongly under the guidance of the Holy Spirit.

**Third,** the evangelical feminist position concerning

Paul leads to a rejection of his authority as an apostle. In writing to the Corinthians about his authority, Paul did speak of his own teaching—but he did not consider the acceptance of his teachings as optional (1 Cor. 11:1–2; 14:33–38). It appears that modern-day feminism falls into the Corinthian error of considering some of Paul's teachings purely optional.

**Fourth,** evangelical feminists insist that all of Paul's passages on women are in practical contexts except for Galatians 3:28, which is theological. One feminist work proclaims, "Of all the passages concerning women in the New Testament, only Galatians 3:28 is in a doctrinal setting; the remainder are all concerned with practical matters."[8] Their conclusion, then, is that Galatians 3:28 is a more important passage for this issue than any other of Paul's writings. Whether or not this is true, their major mistake is in trying to isolate the theological from the practical in Paul's arguments. Duane Dunham observes concerning this fallacy:

> The fact is, that Galatians is not completely doctrinal and 1 Corinthians and 1 Timothy completely practical. Anyone who knows the style of the apostle Paul . . . will remember that he characteristically sets forth his doctrine, then brings the practical implications out of that. Further, his reason for writing the letter to the Galatians was a practical and a theological one. Our practice is solidly built upon our theology, and so was his. The problem of circumcision—practical—arose because of the misunderstanding of the relationship between Law and Grace, and the one concomitant warning this did theological.[9]

**Fifth,** evangelical feminists wrongly assume Galatians 3:28 teaches that any and all order or authority structure in the church should be eliminated because all are one in Christ. That issue is entirely beside the point being discussed. This passage does not advocate doing away with structure and distinction in society; its concern is the subject of justification and the believer's relationship to the Abrahamic covenant. Paul wasn't seeking to demonstrate social equality among the classes he mentioned; instead he wished to show that all, *regardless of standing in society,* may participate by faith in the inheritance of Abraham and become sons of God. To draw social implications from Galatians 3:28 is to go beyond the text.

### Did Paul contradict Christ?

There can be little argument against Christ's high view of womanhood. Albrecht Oepke writes, "We never hear from the lips of Jesus a derogatory word concerning woman as such. In holding out the prospect of sexless beings like that of angels in the consummated kingdom of God . . . He indirectly lifts from woman the curse of her sex and sets her at the side of man as equally the child of God."[10] Even Jewett, in his discussion of Luke 10:38–42, recognizes Jesus' high view of woman.[11]

So then, should we see Paul as the betrayer of Christ in reference to women? Some believe Paul sought greater conformity with the Jewish view of women rather than following Christ's new freedom. For example, Richardson says that Paul "has not pushed Jesus' new view of women any further, but has rather retreated, in the face of local factors that threaten the stability of the struggling community of believers, to a more Judaic and rigidly Pharisaic view."[12] Mollenkott adds that "Jesus doesn't seem to matter much to traditional evangelicals; Paul is the one who counts."[13]

But was Christ's perception of women really contradictory to Paul's? Though Jesus treated women with kindness and respect and considered them equal before God, the biblical record says nothing at all about Christ considering a woman's role in ministry leadership or spiritual headship indistinguishable from a man's.

There is no evidence that any woman was commissioned as one of the seventy or of the twelve. In fact, since the twelve were men, and culturally we may legitimately assume the seventy were men, the burden of proof lies with the person who wants to find women among the seventy commissioned by Jesus. Women were not represented among the apostles who will head the heavenly rule of Christ to come in the New Jerusalem. No amount of argument or rhetoric can change these facts.

How, then, does Paul compare to Christ in his attitude toward women? The Book of Acts and Paul's letters reveal the tender heart Paul had toward women and his appreciation for their help in the gospel ministry. But nowhere did he ordain them as overseers, nor did they serve as apostolic representatives to the churches. Richardson is correct: Paul *has* gone no further than Jesus, and neither should believers today. There is no tension between Christ and Paul concerning order and equality as based on creation.

### Did Paul misunderstand the Old Testament?

The final problem presented by evangelical feminism concerns Paul's alleged misinterpretation of the creation narrative in his counsel on women in 1 Corinthians 11 and 14 and in 1 Timothy 2. Some think God originally intended identical roles for men and women, but the curse (Gen. 3:16) brought women into enslavement. Acceptance of Christ, therefore, brings an end to this curse in the lives of believers. In this view, Genesis 1:27 is seen as teaching the simultaneous creation of male and female, with the result that the two are identical in function as well as essence. The authority of Genesis 2, which presents woman as created after man, is nullified.

Proponents of this view believe Paul correctly interpreted Genesis 1 in Galatians 3:28, but drew improper conclusions from Genesis 2 concerning the subordination of woman to man. Scanzoni and Hardesty, in *All We're Meant to Be* (p. 28), take this position in their discussion of 1 Corinthians 11:8–9. They write, "The second creation narrative does say that woman was made from and for man, but the theological leap from this to woman's subordination is a traditional rabbinic . . . understanding that is not supported by the text."

That brings up the crucial question: Who has misinterpreted Genesis 1 and 2—Paul, or some modern feminists? To answer that, we need to consider several things.

First, Genesis 1:26–28 has nothing to say about social relationships between male and female. It speaks of the essential unity of male and female as image-bearers of God. From this passage Paul concluded that both have an equal right to the grace of God (Gal. 3:28). Moreover, the text does not say male and female were created simultaneously as some feminist scholars have claimed. There is no time frame given in Genesis 1 as there is in Genesis 2.

Second, Genesis 2 indicates that God first created male, and then created female. This is true whether one takes the details literally or figuratively. The woman was to be a helper (not a slave) to the man, corresponding to him. When Adam named her—a prerogative in the Old Testament of one having authority[14]—he demonstrated his authority over her. Paul's teaching, based on the order of creation, indicates man's responsibility for the woman, which is to be carried out with sacrificial love (Eph. 5:22–33). The woman's corresponding responsibility is to follow his leading willingly. These essential, biblically defined roles stem from God's creation, not from man's fall (1 Cor. 11:8–9; 1 Tim. 2:12–14).

Third, Genesis 3:16 does not introduce the hierarchy of male and female. That structure is found in the creation narrative of Genesis 2. The Genesis 3 passage reveals a distortion of the original pattern. Rather than man lovingly ruling and woman willingly submitting, the war of the sexes had begun. Man would seek dominance, with woman vying for his position. This conflict, *not* the divinely created order of authority, is gradually to be done away with in Christ (Eph. 5). Man is to love as he leads, and woman is to submit herself to her husband. In Christ the creation intentions for male and female are restored. Paul understood this truth and carried it over into his teachings on the roles of men and women in the church.

## CONCLUSION

For those of us who hold to a view of the Bible as God's perfect and complete revelation to man, inerrant and infallible, it is clear that Jesus' teachings were a fulfillment of the Old Testament, not a negation. Furthermore, Paul's instruction concerning women's role in church ministry was neither self-contradictory nor inconsistent with Christ's teaching or the Old Testament.

## CHAPTER TWO

# Feminist Interpretations of Scripture

Another feminist position has emerged in recent days. It is championed by evangelical feminists who hold to a high view of Scripture as well as many of the basic tenets of feminism. To its credit, this position has thus far avoided many of the doctrinal aberrations found in non-evangelical and liberal feminism. The ways in which many evangelical feminist scholars and authors have sought to justify their interpretations of specific biblical texts, however, is disturbing. Their methods of interpretation—adopting novel views of the meanings of words and of grammatical and textual factors—if used in other areas of theology would probably be considered forced, if not clearly erroneous. Yet these are their methods of choice.

## WHEN DOES A WORD NOT MEAN WHAT IT SAYS?

Three very important words regarding male and female roles in the church have been redefined by contemporary evangelical feminists. They are the Greek words for *head, submission,* and *exercising authority.* It is important to understand that these terms are used by the apostle Paul in passages defining female and male *functional relationships* in the home and in the gathering of believers, *not* in describing their *personhood and equality* before God.

The Greek word for *head* has traditionally been understood to express authority. For example, Frederik Grosheide says that *head* is used figuratively as "a governing, ruling organ."[1] In recent years, however, several feminists[2] and other scholars[3] have decided that the word carries the idea of "source" or "origin." Obviously, adopting a modified interpretation such as this serves their cause very well, but is the interpretation biblically accurate? And how, we might ask, did this new definition arise?

Several years ago Stephen Bedale wrote an article on the meaning of *kephale*. He suggested that the term would never have been understood by readers of the New Testament as meaning "authority," since this idea was not present in the Greek literature of the time: "In normal Greek usage, classical or contemporary, κεφαλή [*kephale*] does not signify 'head' in the sense of ruler, or chieftain, of a community,"[4] he wrote. He made his claim, however, without one piece of specific evidence; nor did he come to grips with the overwhelming evidence that *head* does express the idea of authority.

In "The Classical Concept of *Head* as 'Source'" (*Equal To Serve*, Appendix III, pp. 267–283), Catherine Kroeger sought to provide a number of examples to prove that *kephale* may mean "source." She prefaced her paper with a quote from a 16th century Latin-Greek lexicon to demonstrate that a dictionary other than Liddell and Scott's classical Greek lexicon allows for a meaning of "source." Because this lexicon listed the meaning for *kephale* as "the *beginning* of the body's stature" [italics mine], Dr. Kroeger saw evidence for a reading of "source."[5] But "the beginning of the body's stature" clearly speaks not to the head as the "source" of the body but as the extremity or starting point of the body. In other words, the head is the topmost extremity just as the feet are the bottom extremity.

The Bedale assessment of *kephale* is decisively disproved by the thorough and penetrating work of Wayne Grudem, who documented over 2,000 instances of *kephale* in all the major writings of the classical and Hellenistic Greek periods.[6] There is virtually no question that *head* conveyed the idea of "authority" or "leader" in

New Testament times and before. Moreover, there is little if any evidence it ever meant "source."[7] In fact, Bedale himself never offers any valid extra-biblical evidence to support his argument.

Words are not fluid; we must view them within the context or parameter of larger meaning. Feminists have sought to invest the Greek word for *head* with a meaning that is not found in the ancient world and has no relationship whatsoever to its root meaning. Anthony Thiselton rightly argues, "Words or other linguistic signs have no 'force,' validity, or meaning, independently of the relations of equivalence and contrast which hold between them."[8] So, when seeking to examine the meaning of a term like *kephale*, we need to be aware that words do not have unlimited meaning. Just like the words we use in everyday speech, Greek terms from the New Testament are confined within the limits of a larger meaning.[9] The following graph illustrates this idea:

The general meaning of a particular word is known as the *normal* or *natural* meaning. This is the most common use of the term. This general meaning is also known as the "unmarked" meaning. That is, it is the meaning one would assume apart from contextual indicators of a meaning other than the general meaning.[10] For *kephale*, the common or unmarked meaning is "the physical head." From that meaning come other meanings such as capital punishment (losing one's head), the prominent part of something (as the head is to the body),[11] or the ruler of something or someone (as the head is of the body). The varied meanings of "head" can easily be seen in the following chart:

## CLASSICAL AND PATRISTIC DICTIONARIES ON *HEAD (KEPHALE)*

### 1.–Liddell, Scott, Jones, McKenzie (Classical)

Head of man or beast; as the noblest part, for the whole person; life (capital punishment); of things, extremity, top or brim of a vessel; in the plural, source of a river, crown or completion, consummation.[12] [Note the very restricted use of the term as "source."]

### 2.–Lampe (Patristic)

Of men or animals: with prepositions, upside-down, head downwards, on one's head, etc.

Life, in the sense to lose one's life (head), as in capital punishment. Metaphorically: of things, main dish, helping of food, a child's toy; of persons, head of the house, chief, headman, religious superior; or bishops; of Christ, head of creation; of the Church.[13]

# IDEA OF *HEAD* IN EXTRA-BIBLICAL GREEK

The head served as the primary figure for leader since for most Greek-speaking peoples at least up through the time of the New Testament the head was the leading faculty of thought, as is evidenced by the following examples:

**Aristotle's** *opinion that intelligence was in the heart "was contrary to the views of some of his medical contemporaries, contrary to the popular view, and contrary to the doctrine of [Plato's]* Timaeus.*"*[14]

**Plato,** *in describing the parts of the body, wrote of "the* head *which is the most divine part and which reigns* (despoteo) *over all the parts within us."*[15]

**Plutarch,** *a non-Christian Roman who lived in the period of the New Testament (A.D. 46–120) said, "We affectionally call a person 'soul' or 'head' from his ruling parts* (apoton kuriotaton).*"*[16]

**Philo,** *a Jew who was a contemporary of Paul the apostle (30 B.C.–A.D. 45) understood the term* head *as referring to rule: "As the* head *in the living body is the ruling place* (to hegemoneuon tropon), *so Ptolemy became head among kings."*[17]

# NEW TESTAMENT DICTIONARIES
## ON *HEAD (KEPHALE)*

### *1.–Bauer, Ardnt, Gingrich, Danker*

Literal head of man or beast; figurative to denote superior rank of living beings; of things, the uppermost part, extremity, end, point.[18]

### *2.–Cremer*

The part of the body which holds together and governs all the outgoings of life.[19]

### *3.–Heinrich Schlier*

Used for the head or ruler of a society.[20]

### *4.–Thayer*

Metaphorically anything supreme, chief, prominent; of persons, master or lord.[21]

### *5.–K. Munzer*

[In Col. 2:10], expresses the authority of Christ . . . and the corresponding subordination of the church.[22]

The idea of "source" or "origin" for the Greek term *kephale* simply has no clear example in the time of the New Testament. The word carries several meanings at different places in the Greek Scriptures, but the use of the term in referring to Christ is paramount; in fact, the husband's headship in 1 Corinthians 11:3 and Ephesians 5:23 is paralleled with Christ's headship. The meaning of the term in any given context must be the one that reflects the "marking" given to the word by the author.[23]

To sense the meaning of *kephale,* substitute the word "leader" or "ruler" in each of the disputed passages, and then the word "source" or "origin." Clearly "source" or "origin" does not fit the verses in question. The same is true in all other examples of *kephale* in the New Testament. "Source" is a meaning foreign to the word throughout the New Testament,[24] a conclusion verified by every major Greek dictionary concerning the New Testament period. To illustrate this, let us examine the different passages in which *kephale* occurs:

| Passages | Key Indicators | Meaning | |
|---|---|---|---|
| Eph. 1:19–23 | "at his right hand" | leader, lord, ruler | "far above all principality, power," |
| | "put all things under his feet" "*head* over all things" | | |
| Eph. 4:15–16 | "grow up into him" | metaphorical | "whole body fitly joined together" |
| Eph. 5:22–27 | "submit yourselves" | leader, ruler | "subject to Christ, so wives to their husbands" |
| Col. 1:16–18 | "by him all things created" "by him and for him" | leader, ruler, creator | "thrones, dominions" |
| | | (stressing power and preeminence) | "in all things preeminence" |
| Col. 2:10 | "head of all principality/ power" | ruler | |
| Col. 2:19 | "nourished and knit together" | metaphorical | |

Feminist scholars argue an exception to this meaning of *kephale*, especially in 1 Corinthians 11. Because Paul speaks of the woman coming from the man, they claim, surely here *head* means "source." But if this is indeed true, then we must also argue that God is the origin of Christ—which would deny the full deity of Messiah. And since Paul follows the statement with the fact that man also comes from woman, headship as "source" is not at all appropriate, for then woman would also be the head or "source" of man, which is contrary to Paul's point.

The solution to this dilemma is simple: we must understand the meaning of *kephale*, "head," as Paul intended and as the evidence overwhelmingly supports. The term expresses authority.

A second word important to our discussion is *au-thenteo*, found in 1 Timothy 2:12. Some feminists argue that the term means to "dominate" or "lord it over" men in the church. Women, then, are not denied authority over men; they are simply not to dominate men.[25] Catherine Kroeger has even suggested that the term relates to women teaching men to engage in sexual rites.[26]

The word *authenteo* is an *hapax legomenon* in the New Testament—that is, it occurs only once. The lexicon by Bauer (in translation) does allow "domineer" as one of the possible meanings[27] for this term, but "authority" is given first. A major study by George Knight of all the occurrences of the term in extant Greek literature confirms the rendering "have authority" as the natural meaning.[28]

Knight provides a list of the ways in which lexicographers have understood *authenteo*. The meanings include "to have full power or authority over," "to be in power, to have authority," "being master," "to execute authority or exercise authority over," "have the right or power for something or over someone."[29] This analysis has not been refuted, even in the recent work by Leland Wilshire based on new sources available through the *Thesaurus Linguae Graecae* project at University of California at Irvine. This computer project has made available to scholars essentially all the ancient Greek sources for determination of word meanings. In the last paragraph of his study, Wilshire recognizes that the papyri and the basic consistency of the early church fathers appear to buttress Knight's conclusions that *authenteo* means to "exercise authority."[30]

The last word of concern in our discussion is *hupotasso*, meaning "submission." At the annual meeting of the Evangelical Theological Society in 1986 at New Orleans, Catherine Kroeger claimed that this Greek word did not mean "to be under another" but "to be attached to" another. Actually she is partially correct; *hupotasso* does carry this meaning when it refers to a literary piece, but *only* in such cases, never when it refers to persons and never in the middle voice in Greek. The term essentially carries the concept of its root meaning, "to arrange under."

The Greek term for *submission* occurs in several different contexts in the New Testament. It is used concerning submission of wives to husbands, Jesus to his parents (Luke 2:51), slaves to masters (Tit. 2:9; 1 Pet. 2:18), Christians to secular authorities (Rom. 13:1; Tit. 3:11; 1 Pet. 2:18), church members to church leaders (1 Pet. 5:5), believers to God (James 4:7; 1 Cor. 15:28b; Heb. 12:9), and believers to Christ (Eph. 5:24). When Paul spoke of the submission of wives to husbands, he used the middle voice in Greek, indicating that her submission is to be an act of will (Eph. 5:22; Col. 3:18; Tit. 2:5; 1 Pet. 3:1, 5). In other words, women cannot *be submitted.* They must willingly surrender their wills to the will of their husband, who in his turn is to be seeking to surrender his will to God. If Ephesians 5:21 is understood as referring to the mutual submission of husbands and wives to each other, then men are to be submissive to their wives. But note that the submission required for husbands in the context is to love them and provide leadership for them. Even Christ served his disciples; this did not, however, nullify his authority over them.

The words *head, exercise authority,* and *submission* carry no dread to one who properly understands that authority and submission are proper expressions of God's work in the home and the church. These terms reflect the intra-trinitarian relationship of the Father and the Son as well. They do not address the issue of essence, but of relationship.

## ARE SOME PASSAGES ON WOMEN'S ROLES NOT GENUINE?

The predominant text questioned on critical grounds by evangelical feminist scholars is 1 Corinthians 14:33b–35 (1 Corinthians 11:2–16 and 1 Timothy 2:12ff are similarly doubted by numerous non-evangelical scholars).[31] The 1 Corinthians 14 passage is particularly at odds with Paul's more positive view on the status of women as observed in his ministry and in his teaching in Galatians 3:28 and 1 Corinthians 11:2–6.

Most who argue for a feminist view of women's ministries are satisfied to leave the passages intact and explain them in a nontraditional manner. Some feminists, however, have questioned the textual integrity of 1 Corinthians 14:34–35. Gordon Fee's analysis in his commentary on 1 Corinthians probably has influenced more thinking on the validity of this text than any other. Fee argues that verses 34 and 35 were not included in Paul's original letter to the Corinthians. The appearance of these verses in some manuscripts in other places than between 1 Corinthians 14:33 and 36, Fee claims, suggests that verses 34 and 35 are a marginal note or "gloss" which made their way into the present text at some later date.[32] He also contends that the verses do not fit in naturally with the context or flow of 1 Corinthians 14 and that they contrast the instruction in 1 Corinthians 11:2–16 on the role of women in the church.[33]

These objections, while interesting, are not persuasive. Not one shred of manuscript evidence exists which indicates the verses are not original, though Fee is correct in observing they do not occupy the same position in all the manuscripts. But here we can surmise that the textual variants are related to the context problems. In other words, because some scholars consider the placement of the verses suspect or awkward, they assume textual problems as well.

1 Corinthians 14:34–35 are found after verse 40 only in several Western manuscripts and Western church Fathers.[34] These are not substantial witnesses in view of the verses' support in the rest of the ancient texts, which are written in Greek and represent the Alexandrian and Byzantine kind of manuscripts. No manuscripts this author could discover omit the verses altogether. What's more,

the placement of verses 34 and 35 after verse 40 is a distinctive reading found in the Western church of the Roman Empire. The manuscripts cited above are not isolated and can easily be attributed to a single source. Even Zuntz, who apparently rejects the authenticity of the two verses, says that the Western position is "an unsuccessful attempt at removing the hitch," which "witnesses to the early existence of the insertion."[35]

The "hitch" referred to by Zuntz actually gives the traditional reading greater credibility. So does the fact that the Western family includes the verses even though transposing them.[36]

Neither are verses 34 and 35 necessarily inappropriate to the context or flow of the passage. In fact, they continue the thought of the prior verses, speaking further to the problem of proper order in the church meeting, as Héring observes: "The Apostle has just restated the principle of decorum, which must be observed in Church gatherings ([1 Corinthians] 14:33a). So it is quite natural that he should go a step farther and reduce to silence the women who, contrary to Jewish and Greek custom, wished to take part in discussions."[37]

Thus verses 34 and 35 may be seen to fit in with the verses that come just before them, especially if Hurley's thesis on judging the prophets is correct; without Hurley's thesis they seem appropriate in the context. And whether or not the passage contradicts 1 Corinthians 11:2–16 depends upon how one interprets the two sections.

Although verse 33b, "As in all the churches of the saints," does fit awkwardly with the phrase which follows in verse 34, "Let the women keep silent in the churches," we cannot presume that verses 33b–35 are a non-Pauline interpolation. One possibility is that the term *ekklesia* is used differently in the two instances, the second reference applying more specifically to church gatherings than to the body of believers itself.

E. Earle Ellis offers another possibility based on his observation that a writer of the first century usually employed an amanuensis to draft a letter. After the author received this draft, he would add any greeting or additional comments he desired to make. Clearly Paul used an amanuensis for the composition of 1 Corinthians (16:21); he or the amanuensis could easily have added verses 34–35 in the margin of the manuscript.[38] Ellis concludes:

> On this assumption the textual problems of 1 Cor. 14:34–35 are readily resolved. (1) An added marginal note would interrupt the flow of the letter and would probably make for rough edges wherever it might be later incorporated. (2) In transcribing the letter, the scribe or scribes behind the majority textual tradition incorporated the passage after 14:33; those behind the Western 'displacement' thought 14:40 to be a more appropriate point to insert it, and a few others copied the letter and left 14:34–5 in its marginal position. However, no MS lacks the verses and, in the absence of some such evidence, the modern commentator has no sufficient reason to regard them as a post-Pauline gloss.[39]

This understanding certainly is more plausible than and takes more seriously the credibility of Paul's words in verses 34–35 than does Fee's interpretation. Without solid evidence, calling verses 34–35 a non-Pauline interpolation is playing "fast and loose" with the text. Nowhere else, to my knowledge, does Fee completely reject a passage which has a displacement problem but is found in all the manuscripts.

Fee also claims that 1 Corinthians 14:34–35 is in "obvious contradiction to 11:2–16."[40] If we conclude that verse 34 forbids *all* speaking, this is true. If, on the other hand, the verse refers to such activities as tongues-speaking, non-inspired speaking, or judging prophets, as different scholars have suggested,[41] then no contradiction exists.

The preferred understanding of 1 Corinthians 14:34–35 is that the passage is genuine and reflects a Pauline perspective. Admittedly it possesses a "rough textual history," due probably to its inception as a Pauline marginal note (and as such, genuinely inspired) added later to the main text by a scribe.

## DID PAUL REALLY SAY THAT?

Other scholars, in a recent attempt to alleviate the difficulty of Paul's prohibition on women speaking in the Christian gathering, attribute 1 Corinthians 14:34–35 to the Corinthians rather than to Paul. Walter Kaiser is an advocate of this perspective. He concludes that Paul did not compose verses 34 and 35[42] for two reasons. First is the requirement of "silence" in verse 34. Such silence, he believes, is contrary to Paul's teaching in 1 Corinthians 11:2–16.[43] Second, he considers the "law" in verse 34 a reference to rabbinic teaching alone since, he says, no such injunction is found in the Old Testament. He concludes that verses 34 and 35 are statements from the Corinthians themselves—statements which Paul quotes and to which he replies in a sharp rejoinder in verse 36.[44]

First, we will examine the likelihood of verses 34 and 35 being part of a letter from the Corinthians rather than Paul's own words. Second, we will consider whether verse 36 is indeed a sharp rejoinder to Corinthian chauvinism. Last, we will interact with Kaiser's two contentions regarding "silence" and "law."

### A Corinthian or a Pauline Statement?

The apostle knew of the problems within the Corinthian congregation by two means. One was the report from the house of Chloe. From this Christian household, Paul learned about the divisions in the church, the immorality (1 Cor. 5:1–13), the lawsuits against one another (6:1–11), and the sexual promiscuity (6:12–20). Second, Paul apparently heard from the Christians at Corinth themselves, probably in a letter, a number of misconceptions which he then specifically addressed in this first letter to the Corinthian church.

# THE ISSUES PAUL ADDRESSED INCLUDED THE FOLLOWING:

7:1— "It is good for a man not to touch a woman."                    *(Corinthians' comment)*

7:2— "Nevertheless, because of sexual immorality, let each man have his own wife, and let each woman have her own husband."                    *(Paul's response)*

8:1— "We know that we all have knowledge."                    *(Corinthians' comment)*

"Knowledge puffs up, but love edifies."                    *(Paul's response)*

10:23—"All things are lawful for me."                    *(Corinthians' comment)*

> "but not all
> things are
> helpful. . . not
> all things
> edify."          *(Paul's response)*

Other examples are possible, but these are characteristic of those portions of the letter from the Corinthians which Paul included in his letter in order to interact with the local assembly.

Kaiser argues that 1 Corinthians 14:34–35 is another such example of a Corinthian misconception to which Paul retorts in verse 36:

> We conclude that in verses 34b-35 [sic, 34–35] Paul is quoting from the letter sent to him by the Corinthians, just as he had done in 1 Corinthians 6:12, 'all things are lawful for me,' and in 8:8 [?] and 10:23. Such quotations became headings for the new subjects Paul introduced.[45]

This view is highly unlikely. Note that the other Corinthian statements are short and pithy, whereas verses 34 and 35 are lengthy and have intricate argument. Such argument is more characteristically Pauline. Gordon Fee recognizes the difficulties of Kaiser's position when he notes:

> There is no hint in v. 34 that Paul has suddenly taken to quoting them [the Corinthians]; there is no precedent for such a long quotation that is also full of argumentation (two explanatory 'for's'); it presupposes the unlikely scenario that some in the church were forbidding women to speak— and especially that the quotation would come from the same Corinthian letter that is otherwise quite pro-women (see on 7:1–7; 11:2–16).[46]

Second, Paul's use of *epitrepo* is similar here to his use of the term in 1 Timothy 2:12. Third, the comment of

Paul in verse 35 that women are to learn in *silence* and *submission* and *not speak* is similar to the command in 1 Timothy 2:11–12.

Kaiser seeks to bolster his argument with Sir William Ramsay's contention that one may know of the presence of a quotation in Paul's works "whenever (Paul) alludes to their knowledge, or when any statement stands in marked contrast either with the immediate context or with Paul's known views."[47] Ramsay's comment is *not* appropriate here, however, because the understanding of Paul's view is the issue in question, and so the "proof" of the argument is circular. Moreover, the understanding of Paul concerning women's silence in the church as recorded in 1 Timothy 2, several years later, may very well have been his view at the time of the writing of 1 Corinthians.

### Isaiah 14:36—Paul's Answer to a Corinthian Misconception?

Kaiser's next point, that verse 36 is a sharp rejoinder to the Corinthian misconception quoted in verses 34 and 35, centers on his reading of the *What?* in verse 36.[48] Note his argument:

> But the heart of the passage is the Greek term *e*, which introduces 1 Corinthians 14:36. This particle startles us with its vivid forcefulness and its strong negative reaction. As J. H. Thayer pointed out in 1889 (*A Greek-English Lexicon*), *e* with the grave accent may appear 'before a sentence contrary to the one preceding [it]. . . .' Thayer then listed 1 Corinthians 14:36 as an illustration. Therefore, 1 Corinthians 14:36 is hardly a summation of verses 33b–35. Consequently, Paul rejects the quotation of verses 33b–35 [sic, 34–35], apparently cited from the Corinthian letter and rabbinic law: 'What! Did the word of God originate with you, or are you [menmasculine form] the only ones it has reached?'[49]

But Kaiser betrays a misunderstanding of basic Greek grammar and of Thayer's meaning of the Greek term *e*. Thayer's lexicon, is generally viewed as inferior to others such as Liddell-Scott or Bauer's. Had Kaiser been able to support his argument from some other authority, his view would have more credence. But regardless of this, let us look again at Thayer's definition of *é:*

> Used 1. to distinguish things or thoughts which either mutually exclude each other, or one of which can take the place of the other . . . c. before a sentence contrary to the one just preceding, to indicate that if one be denied or refuted the other must stand.[50]

Kaiser fails to understand that "contrary" here does not mean "contradictory." He omits Thayer's explanation of "contrary:" "to indicate that if one [sentence] be denied or refuted the other must stand." The point here is that even if one rejects a statement, one must still see the logic of a subsequent statement that affirms the same idea. In reality there is a blurring between this category of Thayer's definition and his subsection b. category, which says the term may be used "after an interrogative or a declarative sentence, before a question designed *to prove the same thing in another way*"[51] [italics mine].

Is Paul seeking to reject the comment in verses 34 and 35 by means of the statement in verse 36? First of all, Kaiser's point that the clause is introduced by *What* with a grave accent is simply irrelevant. No grammarian or lexicographer makes such a pronouncement on the use of the grave accent in Greek as opposed to any other accent. Moreover, the accenting of these words occurred hundreds of years after the writing of the passage.

But even more important in our examination of this question is the use of the word throughout the New Testament, especially in the letters of Paul. Note a few examples Thayer gives in the preceding quote for the proof of his contention.[52]

> Matt. 20:14 Take what is yours and go your way. I wish to give to this last man the same as to you. 15 [Or; é] Is it not lawful for me to do what I wish with my own things? Or is your eye evil because I am good?
> 1 Cor. 6:15 Do you not know that your bodies are members of Christ? Shall I then take the members of Christ and make them members of a harlot? Certainly not! 16 Or [é] do you not know that he who is joined to a harlot is one body with her? For 'the two,' He says, 'shall become one flesh.'
> 1 Cor. 9:5 Do we have no right to take along a believing wife, as do also the other apostles, the brothers of the Lord, and Cephas? 6 Or [é] is it only Barnabas and I who have no right to refrain from working?
> 2 Cor. 11:6 Even though I am untrained in speech, yet I am not in knowledge. But we have been thoroughly manifested among you in all things. 7 [Or; é] Did I commit sin in humbling myself that you might be exalted, because I preached the gospel of God to you free of charge?

An examination of these usages and of the nature of the known Corinthian quotes used by Paul repudiate Kaiser's argument that verse 36 is a sharp rejoinder to the preceding verses supposedly written by the Corinthians. Had Kaiser simply looked at the examples given by Thayer under his subsection c. category, he would have realized his mistake.

One other error remains in Kaiser's analysis. He indicates by the use of brackets in the quoted passage above that the "you" of verse 36 refers to men who are trying to keep women from speaking. He would have us read the verse thus: "Did the word of God originate with you, or are you *men* the only ones it has reached?" Yet surely Dr. Kaiser knows that a second person pronoun, as is found here, does not have gender distinction. The pronoun refers to *all* to whom he is writing, including women as well as men.

## What does Paul mean by "silence"?

If Paul's admonition in 1 Corinthians 14:34–35 for women to keep silent in the church prohibits *any* verbal utterance—praying, singing, prophesying—then surely the passage *does* contradict verses 2–16 of chapter 11. Fortunately this is not a choice we must make. Though women are clearly allowed to prophesy and pray in 1 Corinthians 11:2–16 and are forbidden to make a sound in 14:34–35, the Greek word for "be silent" is different in the two passages. The word Paul used in 1 Timothy 2:11 means to have a quiet demeanor.

What, then, are the women in 14:34 not to say? They are not to judge or proclaim revelation; but they *are* allowed to be a vehicle of the Holy Spirit's direct communication to the church, as expressed in 11:2–16.

## Is the "law" a rabbinic reference?

Kaiser seeks to identify the "law" in 1 Corinthians 14:34 as rabbinic tradition rather than God's Law, since he finds no such prohibition on women speaking in the public assembly in the Old Testament. He then refers to several rabbinic parallels to the ruling. Merely because the Talmud *does* make such statements, however, does not make Paul's reference to the "law" suspect. Certainly the rabbis were not always wrong. Moreover, many evangelical scholars believe the "law" in verse 34 refers by allusion to Genesis 3:16 or some other portion of the Old Testament.[53] Paul referred to the creation-fall narratives in 1 Corinthians 11:9 and 1 Timothy 2:13–14; there is reason to believe he referred to the same passages here in 1 Corinthians 14.

Kaiser's reading of "law" cannot be substantiated and

in no way detracts from the traditional understanding of these verses: that Paul was expressing his theology against aberrant practices in the Corinthian church, a church which tended to exert, not repress, women's roles, contrary to the practices of Paul and the other churches throughout the empire (1 Cor. 11:16).

## LOCAL CHURCH PROBLEMS OR PRINCIPLES FOR THE WHOLE CHURCH?

A second text often questioned on critical grounds by feminist scholars is 1 Timothy 2:12. Evangelical feminists attempt to countermand the instruction in this verse with two arguments: 1) Paul was responding to a specific problem in the Ephesian church; 2) Paul's prohibition was not against women teaching men, but against women teaching men in a domineering way.

Aída Besançon Spencer, in an article in the *Journal of the Evangelical Theological Society* in 1974, argued that Paul's prohibition in 1 Timothy 2 against women teaching was made in response to a "feminist problem" at Ephesus. According to this view, women were teaching unorthodox doctrine in congregational meetings, leading many Christians astray. Therefore Paul enjoined the women at Ephesus, purely on a temporary basis, to refrain from verbally participating in the meeting of the church.[54] This reading is based at least in part on Paul's use of the term "weak women" for those who were deceived and listened to the wrong persons. Some men reacted to the false teaching occurring at Ephesus by excluding women from any teaching at all.[55] In his response to this specific situation, the theory goes, Paul slowed down the move to full equality he would have otherwise supported.[56]

Philip Payne, too, argues that Paul's prohibition should be understood as temporary and localized rather than as a general restriction. He bases his reading on Paul's use of the present tense "I permit" *(epitrepo)*. Under different circumstances, Payne says, women would be allowed to teach in congregational meetings:

> Since in 1 Tim 2:12 Paul uses his typical verbal form for giving his own personal position (first person singular present active indicative) and since he neither claims that his position is from the Lord nor that the same restrictions on women should apply in all the churches, it would seem to be the most natural reading to understand [epitrepo] in 1 Tim 2:12 as referring to the particular situation in Ephesus to which Paul was speaking without necessarily being applicable in all times and places.[57]

False teaching was indeed taking place at Ephesus. It is difficult to assess, however, its nature and the number of people involved.[58] No evidence exists that women had been teaching in the Christian assembly or that they had been teaching men in any context. Paul was concerned that the Ephesians did not give heed to fables and endless genealogies (1 Tim. 1:4) from persons who desired to be teachers of the law (1 Tim. 1:7). If false teaching had been Paul's concern in verses 2:8–15 of chapter 2, he assuredly would have prohibited men from such teaching too. His emphasis, however, was not on women teaching false doctrines, but on women teaching men.

Furthermore, Paul's instruction regarding women teaching men was not prompted by a specific problem in the church at Ephesus, but rather emerged from his understanding of Genesis 1–3. The statements about idle and gossiping women in 1 Timothy 5:13 and the "weak women" led astray in 2 Timothy 3:6 do not support speculations that these women were propagating false doctrine from which Paul restricted them. Again, Paul was concerned about the spread of false doctrine by anyone, man or woman. Women were restricted from teaching men, however, on theological grounds—the priority of man in creation and the deception of Eve in the fall.[59]

Payne's argument about Paul's use of the present tense—"I do not permit"—also fails to undermine Paul's general prohibition. Unquestionably that phraseology *could* carry the connotation of a temporary injunction—but does it in this context? Paul did not always accompany the use of the first person present active indicative with qualifying phrases when he wrote something other than opinion. In Romans 12:1 he wrote, "I urge you, brothers, in view of God's mercy, to offer your bodies a living sacrifice" (NIV). Paul did not use the first person here to restrict action. Rather, he used it to express personal appeal or authority,[60] which was certainly appropriate, if not demanded, in his letter to Timothy. Stephen Clark observes:

> [Paul] used the first person to back up the ruling with his own authority. 1 Tim. 2:12, then, is analogous to 1 Cor. 11:16 as a passage in which a rule universal to the Christian people is reaffirmed on the basis of the apostle's own personal authority. It is a personal reaffirmation, given by someone with the necessary personal authority to give such a reaffirmation, based upon universal teaching, and contained in a book probably intended to be something like a church order. All the evidence points to the conclusion that this passage has been preserved for us in the canon of scripture as a basic ruling on the roles of men and women in community leadership.[61]

Paul's prohibition of women teaching men was not merely a temporary restriction based on certain problems at Ephesus. Rather, it was a universal prohibition based on God's creative order and the judgment on Eve in the fall.

## DOMINEERING WOMEN

In 1 Timothy 2:12 Paul says that women are not allowed to teach men or to exercise authority over men.

Philip Payne seeks to alleviate this difficulty by contending that the teaching and the exercising of authority are one function rather than two and that Paul's prohibition is not against women teaching men, but of women teaching men in a domineering manner:

> Perhaps the single most crucial question for a proper interpretation of 1 Tim. 2:12 is whether the conjunction [*oude* or *and*] was intended to separate two distinct prohibitions or to join together two parts of one interrelated prohibition. Does it separate two distinct prohibitions, first teaching, and second domineering men? Or does it join together two parts of one interrelated prohibition such as: 'to teach a man in a domineering way?'[62]

In order to prove his thesis, Payne argues that the apostle Paul used this particular Greek conjunction (the "and" between "teach" and "exercise authority") to join together closely related items, to "make specific a single coherent idea,"[63] so that the sense of 1 Timothy 2:12 is, "I am not allowing a woman to teach in a domineering manner."

But Payne's argument about the conjunction *oude* is based on insufficient evidence and is simply inaccurate. The examples he cites for the "single concept" use of this Greek conjunction just do not lead to the conclusion that 1 Timothy 2:12 refers to "teaching in a domineering way." Payne's statement that the two words joined by the conjunction indicate a *single coherent idea* does not follow from his argument that the conjunction joins "two closely related items." The indication (a single coherent idea) may be found in any other examples in Pauline literature. As Thomas Edgar says:

> If the single concept in 1 Tim. 2:12 is authority (specifically the prohibition of women exercising authority over a man) then the construction 'reinforces or makes more specific' the prohibition of

a woman having authority over a man. A study of
*oude* reveals that this is precisely the meaning of the
construction in 1 Tim. 2:12 and that the adjectival or
hendiadys relationship (teach domineeringly, or teach
authoritatively) is incorrect.[64]

An investigation of the 144 New Testament instances
of *oude* in the construction found in 1 Timothy 2:12 reveals that the term is used "for reinforcement or intensification of a concept to which both elements relate"[65]—
*not* to indicate the elements represent a single coherent
idea. For example, "you do not know the day nor the
hour" in Matthew 25:13 does not mean "you do not know
the hourly day," or the "hour type of day," but instead
means "you do not know the day *nor even* the hour." The
second concept "is not eliminated as a separate concept
. . . but reinforces and intensifies the overall thought."[66]

Edgar says that of the 109 non-Pauline uses of *oude*,
only fourteen could be forced into the "single concept"
framework; they are better understood, however, as inten-
sive uses,[67] such as that in Matthew 6:20, "where thieves
neither break in nor steal." Surely these words should not
be understood to mean "where thieves do not make a
stealing type of break-in."[68]

Paul's writings contain thirty-five instances of the conjunction *oude*, and his use of the term is consistent with
non-Pauline usage. 1 Timothy 6:16 is a good example:
Paul writes of God, "who alone has immortality, dwelling
in unapproachable light, whom no man has seen or can
see, to whom be honor and everlasting power" (NKJV).
Edgar comments on this verse:

1 Tim. 6:16 does not appear to mean that no man
has seen God with an 'able to see' type of seeing (but
possibly has some other way); rather the basic
concept, the transcendence of God, is reinforced by
the statement that no one has seen God nor in fact
can see Him.[69]

1 Timothy 6:16, then, has two similar ideas, the latter of which reinforces the former. This is an intensification, not a hendiadys. Such is the proper sense of "I do not permit a woman to teach nor to exercise authority over a man" in 1 Timothy 2:12.

Edgar concludes his study thus: "The evidence is amazingly one-sided. There is not one instance of the [other] 143 occurrences . . . which functions as a hendiadys."[70] The evidence is overwhelming that *oude* is used to join similar ideas and intensify the concepts; special pleading is required to see most if not all the instances of its use, including 1 Timothy 2:12, as examples of single concept hendiadys.[71]

Clearly the passage teaches that women were neither to teach men nor to exercise authority over men. *Teaching* in the early church was the teaching of the Old Testament, and the *authority* expressed in the congregation was ecclesiastical in nature; thus Paul's readers would have understood that the prohibited teaching was the teaching of Scripture and the prohibited authority spiritual authority over men.

## CONCLUSION

Feminist authors and scholars have attempted to undermine the traditional and standard understanding of the roles of men and women in the home and in the church through a variety of methods: giving unusual meanings to words, raising questionable grammatical points, appealing to textual irregularities, and the like. Each of these methods has been found wanting and not worthy of solid biblical and evangelical scholarship. One wonders, since feminists must go to such lengths to prove their points, whether their views are a serious option for the Christian who adheres to the Reformation principle of Scripture alone *(sola scriptura)*.

Certainly many evangelical feminists have weakened the walls of orthodoxy. They have developed an inadequate view of inspiration and an unacceptable method of interpretation. In attempting to make the biblical text speak their language—rather than learning its language—these feminists have woven their preconceived ideas into the Scriptures and fabricated inconsistencies and tensions in Paul's writings which, in reality, never existed in the first place.

Just as unfortunate, their influence has permeated the thought of other scholars who profess a high view of Scripture but are sympathetic to the tenets of feminism and desire to reconcile feminist ideals with an inerrant Scripture.

Each of these groups, as well as those who err on the other end of the spectrum by imposing artificial limits on the avenues of ministry biblically open to women, need to examine anew what God's Word has to say about the proper role of women in the church. Our examination must be undertaken with a heart submissive to the sweeping authority of the Bible, and with a method of interpretation that does not allow the Bible to undermine or contradict itself.

# CHAPTER THREE

# Women in the Time of the New Testament

To understand properly the function and status of women in the early church, we must first comprehend the position they occupied in society as a whole. Then, comparing similarities and contrasting differences, we can see if Christianity made any particular impact on the Mediterranean world, or if it simply maintained the status quo.[1] The societies of Greece, Rome, and Palestine—societies which progressed unevenly in the recognition of women's rights—are those most relevant to our study.

## WOMEN IN GREEK SOCIETY

The road to female emancipation in Greece was hard and long. By the time of the New Testament era, while Roman law and custom had given women considerable freedom, Greek society had made very little progress. Eugenia Leonard observes:

> In Greece the status of women had varied both as to time and place but under most conditions it was inferior to that of men. She was sold practically as a slave to her husband, although she retained partial control of her dowry. She was generally uneducated except in her home responsibilities, took no part in political life and was considered as property whether she was a wife, hetairai, or slave.[2]

54

Historically, the amount of freedom given to women in Greek culture varied from period to period. The women of the heroic age enjoyed considerable social liberty. Consider Sarah Pomeroy's observations:

> Compared with subsequent Greek literature, epic gives a generally attractive impression of the life of women. They were expected to be modest, but were not secluded. Andromache and Helen walk freely through the streets of Troy, though always with escorts, and women are shown on the shield of Achilles helping to defend a city's walls. The rendezvous of a boy and girl outside the walls of Troy is referred to. Wives, notably, Helen, Arete, and Penelope may remain within the public rooms in the presence of male guests without scandal. Not only concubines but legitimate wives are considered desirable, and there is little trace of the misogyny that taints later Greek literature.[3]

Two facts stand out, however, as we evaluate the romanticism of the heroic period. First, the woman's position depended on her husband's success as a warrior and his ability to maintain his family's independence in a highly competitive world. And second, the upper strata of society idealized in epic literature was supported by nameless serfs and semi-free poor people who lived on the edge of starvation and deprivation.[4]

The concept that women are inferior to men is found throughout literature of the time, in the stories about the gods and goddesses and in the treatises of learned men. Hesiod (700 B.C.), for example, saw woman as the agent or embodiment of evil. His negative view of women comes into focus in the story of Pandora, who was responsible, according to Greek mythology, for bringing sin upon mankind.[5]

Herodotus presented a philosophy of male superiority

and the exploitation of women. He appeared for instance, to accept the Illyrian custom of gathering all girls of marriageable age for presentation to men who would purchase them, starting with the most beautiful and ending with the most homely.[6]

Plato is often cited as one who truly considered women to be equal with men. And while it is true he taught that women should be educated on a par with men, such education was for a utilitarian end—namely, that women might be best and most fully used by the state. In the *Republic*, in fact, he propounds his view through the voice of Socrates that both men and women should receive the best possible education for the benefit of the state, even though women are basically inferior to men.[7] Plato also viewed physical love with a woman as inferior to homosexual love, and as solely for purposes of procreation.[8] According to *Laws*, women were bad educators for children because they failed to discipline them.[9] Finally, in Plato's discussion of the origin of women in *Timaeus*, we reach, in one writer's words, "a Platonic low":[10] "On the subject of animals, then, the following remarks are offered. Of the men who came into the world, those who were cowards or led unrighteous lives may with reason be supposed to have changed into the nature of women in the second generation."[11]

Aristotle excelled his teacher in the denigration of women. He saw the inferiority of women as inherent in the sex,[12] and the inequality of man and woman was a permanent part of his thinking.[13]

Women in most periods of Greek history were very much under the dominion of men and lived very secluded lives. Women were prohibited from participating in the non-domestic affairs of life. In fact, so much was this the case that if she were a citizen she was a prisoner in her home. This seclusion apparently was to guarantee that any children she bore would be those of her husband. Charles Ryrie notes:

In Athens . . . the State was all important. All the citizens of Athens were connected by blood ties of some sort, and they took great pains to maintain this relationship. Consequently, careful distinction was made between citizens and strangers and between the offspring of each group. Citizen women, therefore, were forced to lead very secluded lives.[14]

Nevertheless, women were highly honored by their husbands—but ordinarily only within the context of being mothers and housekeepers. In this realm the woman was a ruler and possessed a place of honor, a view Thucydides (5th century B.C.) placed in the mouth of Pericles: "If I am to speak also of womanly virtues . . . I will sum up all in a brief admonition: Great is your glory if you fall not below the standard which nature has set for your sex, and great also is hers of whom there is least talk among men whether in praise or in blame."[15]

Xenophon provided a positive note, but though he viewed man and woman as equals, he also believed men and women had different gifts calling for different roles. In his *Oeconomicus*, Ischomachus says to his wife concerning the vocational differences of man and woman, "And since both the indoor and the outdoor tasks demanded labour and attention, God from the first adapted the woman's nature, I think, to the indoor and man's to the outdoor tasks and cares."[16]

The women of Sparta were the one exception to this secluded way of life, other than that to be discussed below. In Sparta young women were urged to be physically fit and, unlike their counterparts in Athens, were well fed. Menial tasks at home were left for women of inferior class, while citizen women spent their time in the gym and involved with music, household management, and childrearing.[17]

Plutarch reveals the reason for this attention to women: Lycurgus, the legendary giver of the Spartan con-

stitution in the 7th century B.C., encouraged women to be
strong and healthy so they would produce the best possible children. Young women were thus ordered to exercise
regularly by wrestling, running, and participating in other
such sports. Lycurgus saw children as more the property
of the commonwealth than of their parents, and his encouragement of reasonable treatment for women was in
reality an attempt to control them.[18]

His interest in the freedom of women in other words,
was utilitarian, purely for the welfare of the State. Child-
birth was the glory of the woman for the increase of the
population of male warriors, or for girls who would one
day bear male warriors. Consider Plutarch's dialogue between two Spartan women. "Another was burying her
son, when a commonplace old woman came up to her and
said, 'Ah the bad luck of it, you poor woman.' 'No, by
heaven,' said she, 'but good luck, for I bore him that he
might die for Sparta, and this is the very thing that has
come to pass for me.'"[19]

The only women in Athens who had considerable freedom were the *hetairai* (unless it be prostitutes, who, however, were harassed at different periods of Greek history).
Scanzoni and Hardesty say:

> Since it was considered improper to take one's wife
> out in public, men often found intellectual female
> companionship from among the *hetairai* (the word
> means "companion," "girl friend," or "mistress").
> Artistic, cultured, often well educated and
> intellectual, the *hetairai* were free to do as they
> pleased and were treated essentially as equals by
> men. Many of the Greek scholars had mistresses
> from among these women; and it was common
> custom for a married man to invite a *hetairai* to
> attend a social gathering with him. Men admired the
> talents and highly cultivated minds of these women,
> whom Seltman describes as generally having been
> "foreigners from other Greek states and cities,

earning a living sometimes in commerce: business girls, bachelor girls, models." Because they were considered courtesans, however, they were not free to marry Greek citizens. They lived on the fringes of society, free from family obligations (and the seclusion this meant for Greek women).[20]

Plutarch spoke of a "companion" of Pericles, one Aspasia, to whom Pericles was faithful until his death, though being unable to marry her because of Athenian law. She was an intimate friend of Socrates, Phidias, Anaxagoras, Sophocles, and Euripides, discussing often with them on a multitude of subjects.[21]

Though the *hetairai* enjoyed greater mobility than citizen women, the latter had more protection under the law. Lacey observes:

> In law . . . the Athenian married woman had an economic security not enjoyed even by the modern married woman; her property was securely settled on her, and if she left her matrimonial home, as she could do if she wanted, her husband had to return her property or pay interest on it; if she did not leave her home, her husband had to support her. Granted, this was no guarantee against her being made penniless if her husband lost his all and died, but there was protection against the wayward husband of the modern divorce-courts who could support his family but refuses to do so.[22]

With the coming of Alexander of Macedon (336–323 B.C. regnum) also came a greater measure of freedom for women. E. M. Blaiklock points out that "Macedonian inscriptions bear witness to the respected and responsible position of women in the modern Greek communities."[23]

Ryrie adds:

> After the time of Alexander the Great, women began to have a relatively greater measure of freedom.

This was especially true in Macedonia, and was due largely to the fact that Macedonian dynasties produced an extra-ordinary succession of able and masterful women such as Arsinoe, Berenice, and Cleopatra. These women played a large part in civic affairs, for they "received envoys . . . built temples, founded cities, engaged mercenaries, commanded armies, held fortresses, and acted on occasion as regents or co-rulers." What is more important is that from the courts of Macedonia came relative freedom to those women who desired emancipation. They could be educated, take part in club life, appear at the games, and in general enjoy freer relations with men. Nevertheless, "most of these things clearly relate only to a minority. Freedom was not automatic, but had to be grasped; education for the mass was rudimentary, and even in the first century there were women, rich enough to own slaves, who could neither read nor write. Greece suffered from the sexes being on different levels of culture."[24]

The opportunity for women to express themselves publicly and to receive deserved recognition was sparse from archaic through Hellenistic times. The rule of priestesses alongside priests in Greek religion offered some relief in this area.[25] More important is the literary work of several women, most notably Sappho of Lesbos, a poetess whose work attracted such disciples as Catullus, Horace, Ovid, and many down to the modern period.[26] Finally, there was the praise of Herodotus for Artemisia, who led a large part of the Persian force against Greece.[27]

## WOMEN IN ROMAN SOCIETY

The lot of women changed considerably from the days of the early Roman Republic to those of the later Roman Empire. In earlier days, the wife and daughter had little power, economically, domestically, or politically; during the late Republic and early Empire, however, changes in the family gave women access to all these areas of life.

Unfortunately, these changes were not without a cost—the destruction of the Roman family, affected by the same social adjustments that gave freedom to women. During the Archaic period of Rome's history, the right of the father over his wife and children was granted to him by the Twelve Tables.[28] The *pater familias* had absolute authority over his wife and children, extending to the right of the husband to divorce his wife, marry his daughter to a man other than one she would choose, or make his daughter leave her husband. He even held the power of life and death over his family.[29] This power of the father continued over male children until the death of the father,[30] but for wives and daughters it continued even after the man's death under the auspices of the nearest male relative of legal age, or of a guardian designated by the man in his will.[31]

The wife and daughter were regarded as children before the law, and thus under the tutelage of males, because according to Roman philosophy, women were weak and light-minded.[32] When the daughter married, she usually passed from her father's care and authority to her husband's. It was, however, the decision of her *pater familias*. If he chose to transfer his power to the husband, the woman then came under the authority of her husband's *pater familias*. If her marriage did not allow for this transfer of power, the bride was not a legal member of her husband's family,[33] but was still under her father's care.

The purpose of the father having such power was to maintain the family, the cornerstone of Roman social structure. The Roman state was perceived as an association of households, and a person's position in a household determined his status in the community. The household included the head of the household, his wife, his sons and their wives and children, any unmarried daughters, and the household slaves. A strong parallel existed between the power of the head of the household over his dependents and of the power of the community over the citizens.[34]

We should not assume that the arrangement discussed above was intolerable. It is clear that affectionate relationships existed in the Roman household. In addition, there was room for difference of opinion, as illustrated in *The Persian* by Plautus (254?–184 B.C.). In this work the daughter of Saturio attempts to reason with her father over some improper business affairs, trying to dissuade him from using her in a deception. Finally, however, she submits to his wishes.[35]

Even with the relative freedom of women as compared to Greek society, one must remember that hatred of women was very real in Roman society. Dio Chrysostom relates a practice of the Roman city of Tarsus, where women would entirely cover their bodies from sight except for a slit for their eyes. The custom, he says, was a remnant of a chastity that no longer existed. Women were viewed as impure: "They walk with their faces covered, but with soul uncovered, and indeed wide open."[36]

At any rate, the "head of household" system began to weaken after the Second Punic War. In order to strengthen the family estates, dowry rights were kept under the authority of the father rather than passing to the husband at marriage. This tended to give the woman more control of her property and thus more independence in marriage. After this it even became possible for a woman to divorce her husband, although she was still under the paternal authority.

In time, women began to gain power and wealth. They were allowed to inherit, make legal contracts and wills, and initiate divorce.[37] Augustus, seeking to encourage a greater birthrate, encouraged more freedom for women. The free woman who bore three children or the freedwoman who bore four was exempted from a male guardian.[38] This decree helped reverse the negative attitude toward women, as noted by Pomeroy: "This provision incidentally impaired the juridicial [sic] doctrine of the weakness of the female sex, by expressing the notion that at least those women who had demonstrated responsible behavior by bearing the children Rome needed could be deemed capable of acting without a male guardian."[39]

By the time of the late Republic, guardianship was considered burdensome and rarely deterred women from acting on their own initiative. Women such as Cornelia and Terentia were apparently unimpaired in making legal and financial decisions, never consulting a guardian.[40] By Hadrian's day women could, without hindrance, draft a will or make decisions on marriage.[41]

The laws concerning guardianship were certainly instrumental in encouraging female emancipation. When various philosophers and moralists began to raise the question of the equality of women and men, the idea of equal treatment was fostered even more. Stoicism, first taught by Zeno of Greece, was advocated by Seneca, Epictetus, and the emperor Marcus Aurelius, who all urged elevation of the position of women.

The philosopher Musonius Rufus may have provided the most significant thinking on the equality of women with men. He advocated equal education for girls and boys. Moreover, he saw marriage as a reciprocal relationship; husbands and wives were to care for one another in sickness and in health for all time. In addition, he believed men should live by the same sexual code they expected of women.[42]

Various religions of the time allowed and encouraged women to participate, which heightened their consciousness and recognition.[43] Many writers of the time feared that the growing emancipation of women would bring deterioration of morals and the destruction of the family.[44] Certainly women did begin to be more lax in their morals with added freedom,[45] as evidenced by a quote from Seneca (in A.D. 54): "Is there any woman that blushes at divorce now that certain illustrious and noble ladies reckon their years, not by the number of consuls, but by the number of their husbands, and leave home to marry, and marry in order to be divorced?"[46]

Such vices were not, however, restricted to women, for even such men as Cicero and Cato were guilty of divorcing their wives for greater wealth. But it seems that a passion for a lack of responsibility developed in the move toward women's emancipation. "To live your own life," was the movement slogan: "So that you may do what you choose and indeed so I can indulge myself. It is permitted for you to shout and mix the sea and heavens! To be human!"[47]

## WOMEN IN JEWISH SOCIETY

The status of women in Judaism appears to have been a paradox. Sometimes they were afforded considerable praise, but at other times they were denigrated. Note, for example, Proverbs 31, probably unexcelled in the ancient world in its praise of women. A truly "liberated" woman is extolled by husband, children, and community in this passage.

Additionally, man and woman were held equally responsible, in the opinion of R. Johanan b. Baroka (ca. A.D. 120–140), to be fruitful and multiply as Genesis 1 commands.[48] The paradox may be solved by recognizing that women were held in high esteem, but only in their proper sphere (though Proverbs 31 seems to imply much more). That sphere, says Ryrie, was the home, while public affairs were for men.[49]

This attitude is well illustrated by the fact that in the synagogue after the men prayed, "Blessed art thou, O Lord our God, king of the universe, who hast not made me a woman,"[50] women were to pray, "Blessed art thou, O Lord our God, King of the Universe, who has made me according to thy will."[51] Often Jewish women were viewed negatively and considered inferior to men, but apparently a necessary evil.

Bonsirven says that misogyny was widespread in Israel. He claims this hatred of women is found in Proverbs and Ecclesiastes, but is much harsher in Ecclesiasticus. Judaism depreciated the intelligence and virtue of woman because sin came through her and she was more or less given to witchcraft.[52] This attitude is exemplified in a portion from the *Testament of Reuben:*

> *Pay no heed to the face of a woman,*
> *Nor associate with another man's wife,*
> *Nor meddle with affairs of womankind.*[53]

These words are in the context of Reuben's sin with Bilhah; woman is seen as the seducer.

The inferiority of women was a clearly represented idea in the thoughts of several important persons and movements in the first century A.D. Philo, (who was most likely somewhat biased, however), claimed the Essenes sought to do away with the problem of women in their midst. He wrote, "For no Essene takes a wife, because a wife is a selfish creature, excessively jealous and . . . adept at beguiling the morals of her husband and seducing him by her continued impostures [charms]."[54] Philo doubtless was wrong about the Essenes totally rejecting marriage, however, and he went far beyond anything implied in the Dead Sea Scrolls, in my opinion, as to Essene feeling about women.[55]

Philo himself entertained a clearly chauvinistic view of women, and though he did not speak for all Jews, he was without question a devout Jew of considerable influence. Though he was willing to find virtues in some women,[56] he "saw woman in a role strictly secondary to man, inferior and subordinate."[57]

Josephus was less biased against women than Philo, but he still reflected an attitude of male superiority. He tended to stereotype women throughout his writings, characterizing them in negative terms. In the story of Joseph, Josephus says, Potiphar's wife acted in a "womanly fashion" when she avenged herself at his refusal of her.[58] In another place Josephus referred to Antipater's mother as speaking to certain people "in the frivolous way of woman."[59]

The denigration of women in general, at least in the

non-domestic realm, severely limited their freedom and privileges. A woman found her identity as a member of a family—daughter, wife, mother—rather than as an individual. The woman had no recourse to divorce[60] and her property rights were meager. She would inherit property only if there were no sons. Women were unable to defend themselves, to any appreciable degree, in court.[61]

Educational opportunities for women by the time of Christ is uncertain. Apparently some women were educated at least in religious issues, as Lois, Eunice, and Priscilla were. But the opportunities may have been greater for Jewish women in the Hellenistic world than in Palestine proper. If a knowledge of the Old Testament as seen in Mary's song in Luke 1:46–55 is also indicative of the learning of Jewish girls in Palestine, the education of girls may have been very acceptable.

The role of Jewish women in society was almost totally domestic, however. Philo believed that by nature women were more suited to indoor life and men to outdoor life. A woman was to avoid the streets, avoid the gaze of men, and visit the temple only when most people had gone home.[62]

At a later time the Talmud summed up the purpose of a woman in marriage: "grind corn, suckle children, be a beautiful wife and bear children."[63] Even in Hellenized cultures, the strong family center did not allow the freedom of women to increase significantly. Women were not totally excluded from the outside work force in Jewish history, however, as evidenced by Anna in Tobit 2:11–12 and the woman of Proverbs 31.

Lest this description of woman's place in Jewish society become one-sided, we must realize that women did have moments of considerable freedom and dignity both outside and inside the home. Women such as Sarah, Esther, Deborah, and Ruth provided Old Testament models for Jewish women of later years. During the post-biblical period of Judaism, heroines such as Judith, who delivered Israel, and an unnamed mother who courageously died

with her seven sons under the tyranny of Antiochus
Epiphanes (2 Maccabees 7) also supplied women with
models to emulate.

Ryrie comments on the dignity of woman as wife and
mother at that time:

> In the home the Jewish woman's position was one
> of dignity and responsibility. She was her husband's
> conscience charged with the task of encouraging him
> in all holiness. Children, who were a sign of the
> blessing of God on a home, were the special charge of
> the mother. It seems to have been the general practice
> that the mother named the children. As the children
> grew older it became the woman's holy vocation to
> assist in their training, for the first teaching would
> naturally devolve on the mother. And yet in this
> training she did not act alone, for the father joined
> her in a coordinate relationship, and equal reverence
> to both parents was expected from the children. Thus
> in this regard, at least, a Jewish mother fulfilling her
> responsibilities in the sphere of her home receives
> equal honor with the father. . . . Subordination,
> subjection, dignity, and responsibility correctly
> describe the various aspects of the private life of a
> Hebrew woman, but in the sphere of the home her
> place was beyond question a prominent one.[64]

What of women in respect to Jewish religious life? Ex-
odus 38:8 provides the earliest allusion to women participating in public worship, serving at the door of the
tabernacle. Though women could not function as priestesses in Israel (possibly due to periodic menstruation,
which made them ceremonially unclean), they were part
of the covenant community.[65]

Evelyn and Frank Stagg quote Josephus to the effect
that women were restricted to the court of the woman in
the temple.[66] Whether or not this was a consistent practice is uncertain, since both Mary and Joseph are pictured

as bringing the sacrifice to the priests at the end of her purification period (Luke 2:22–38), which may indicate she entered beyond the outer court in the temple area.

Louis Epstein contends there was no separation of the sexes in the First Temple and no special place set aside for women. In the Second Temple there was the *Ezrat Nashim*, the women's court, but even this was so named because women were usually sent there and did not enter into the inner court for a sacrificial rite. In fact, the *Ezrat Nashim* was a public court that both males and females used, where even the male Jew remained when not involved in the inner court.

Three facts suggest this court was not a means to segregate the men from the women: 1) It was used for general public worship for men and women; 2) It was many times the section designated for males, so it could not have been for women only; 3) A number of the chambers used in temple functions opened to this court, and the gate into the court was the most popular entrance for males passing to the section reserved for Israelites and Levites.[67]

## CONCLUSION

The status of women varied in the cultures of Greece, Rome, and Palestine according to various social and legal movements in the history of the Mediterranean world. One thing seems clear: even if women were at times given legal protection and opportunity, including many, if not most, of the privileges enjoyed by men, they never fully achieved recognition as equal persons in every respect to men.

## CHAPTER FOUR

# Ministry of Women in the New Testament

## JESUS AND THE MINISTRY OF WOMEN

Jesus demonstrated a concern and love for humanity unmatched by any other figure in history. God, in the garden, had stamped man with His image. Now He reentered His creation to redeem man from sin. Unlike most of his contemporaries, Jesus looked upon all classes of people with compassion, offering love and forgiveness. The outcasts of society—the sick, publicans, prostitutes, women—were given special favor.

In the pivotal biblical event of the incarnation, two women, Mary and Elizabeth, were primary characters in whom and through whom the drama unfolded. Each displayed an exemplary faith in the covenant promises of God, and each was privileged with the personal revelation of God. Moreover, Mary merited mention at the beginning of Christ's public ministry, the miracle at the wedding in Cana of Galilee, and her welfare was of concern to the Savior even as he hung on the cross.

In John 4, Christ not only violated several social taboos by conversing with a woman who was also a Samaritan and an adulteress, but He revealed to her His identity as the Messiah. Christ's relationship with Mary and Martha likewise broke with social convention as He took the time and effort to converse with them about the spiritual significance of their actions and attitudes. Our Lord defended a woman who expressed her repentance with tears and expensive ointment, was understanding toward a woman with a chronic hemorrhage and saving faith, and was attentive to the Syrophoenician woman who recognized God's Messiah.

The Staggs, in *Woman in the World of Jesus*, also cite the woman bent double (Luke 13:10–17), a widow of Nain (Mark 5:39), the widow's offering (Mark 12:41–44), the woman caught in adultery (John 7:53–8:11), and women who ministered with Jesus as other examples of Christ's openness and acceptance of women as equal with men in the community of faith.

Stephen B. Clark, in *Man and Woman in Christ* (pp. 241–242), writes:

We can contrast Jesus with the rabbis as seen in the Talmud and Midrash. Jesus did not behave the same way. Women come to him and he helps them directly. He heals them (Mark 5:25–34). On occasion he touches them (Matt. 8:14–15). He talks to them individually, regularly in private and sometimes in public (John 11:17–44). On one occasion he even talks to a woman when both of them were unaccompanied (John 4:7–24). He teaches women along with the men (Luke 10:38–42). When he teaches, he speaks of women and uses womanly tasks as illustrations. On occasion, he makes use of two parables to illustrate the same point, one drawn from the activities of men, the other from the activities of women (Luke 15:3–10). He never shows disrespect to women, nor does he ever speak about women in a disparaging way. He relates in a brotherly fashion to women whom he knows. He has some women traveling with him to serve him (Luke 8:1–3). Finally, he calls women "daughters of Abraham" (Luke 13:16), explicitly according them a spiritual status like that accorded to men. One might add here that after his resurrection Jesus appears to women first and lets them carry the news to the men (John 20:11–19; Matt. 28:9–10).

## Breaking Social Conventions

As we have already seen, social conventions of the day did not allow a man to have social interaction with a woman except in a few limited contexts. Primarily the woman stayed in the home; it was considered improper for a man to speak with a woman in public or to touch a woman. Jesus broke both standards.

Our Lord, in fact, broke not only with social conventions but with religious (though not necessarily scripturally prescribed) mores and conventions. In Christ's day, women were neither required nor forbidden to study the Law. Even so, it was rare that a woman would be well-versed in formal religious argumentation or equipped for intelligent religious debate. Thus women were not expected to participate in religious criticism and interaction, and we can assume the woman who did so would face a certain amount of ridicule or bias. This, however, did not prevent Christ from interacting with women on a deep, intensely personal as well as intensely orthodox level.

The typical Jewish male's view of women at the time of Christ cannot be accurately ascertained, since most of the preserved documentation represents rabbinic thought rather than that of the masses. But because of the authoritative influence of rabbinic teaching on the lives of all Jewish men, what has been preserved undoubtedly represents a high percentage of popular thought of the time.

Within this context, a woman's knowledge of the Law was assumed to be minimal. (An exception to this would be the marital requirement that wives be well-versed in Mishnaic requirements concerning domestic duties and the centrality of the home.) Yet Christ revealed no such assumption in His interaction with women.

Another assumption of at least part of the male Jewish population was that women were less intelligent or more easily deceived than men. Aída Besançon Spencer, in *Beyond the Curse*, notes: "First century Jews . . . differed on whether women were more easily deceived than men. Philo explains in *The Embassy of Gaius* that: 'the judgments of women as a rule are weaker and do not apprehend any mental conception apart from what their senses perceive' (XL [319])." This idea was not universally the case, as Spencer notes, but it was prevalent enough to become the source of rabbinic debate and no doubt influenced the way women were treated in the religious community. Again, however, we see no such assumption held by Christ during His earthly life and ministry. His questions to women and His responses to their answers, in fact, seem to reveal an assumption of equal intelligence, equal spiritual discernment, and equal religious acumen.

All of this is not to say that Christ's interaction with women was a source of continual controversy and surprise. As Clark has pointed out (p. 245):

> The simplest and most striking fact . . . in examining Jesus' approach to women is the lack of apparent controversy created by it. The evidence—mostly from the gospels—indicates that his relations to women never caused the same kind of surprise and concern as did his relations to tax collectors and sinners. On one occasion, when he seemed to be acting toward a woman in a way that was deemed improper (his conversation with the Samaritan woman in John 4:27), the surprise shown by his disciples indicates that the incident was an exceptional event in Jesus' life. The most likely interpretation of the disciples' words would be that Jesus did not normally speak to women in public in the way he did with the Samaritan woman. While much is made of the fact that Jesus felt freer to speak with and deal with women than the scribe-rabbis did, it is not often observed that at the same time women in the gospel writings also felt freer to approach Jesus than would be expected if the customs portrayed in the Talmudic writings were the common Jewish

practice at this time. One is dealing, in other words, with a freer situation altogether. The evidence indicates that Jesus' normal behavior with regard to women was not understood to be revolutionary by people in his environment.

Did Jesus break with social convention in the treatment He afforded women during His earthly ministry? The answer is a resounding "Yes!" Was His interaction with women totally outside the realm of acceptable behavior? We have to conclude it was not. It was notable, it was unusual, and it was representative of a higher view of women than was allowed by some (if not a majority) of rabbinic authorities. But it was not indicative of a social revolution. It was, as was His interaction with publicans, sinners, and the "unclean" of His day, the outworking of the spirit of the Law in the Person of Messiah.

## Why were not Women made Apostles?

In light of Christ's willingness to cross over accepted, even rigid, lines of social decorum and to violate outright taboos, a troublesome question emerges: Why did not Christ select any women, or even one woman, as an apostle?

If indeed the Lord broke down pseudo-spiritual "fences" the rabbinic teachers had built around valid points of the Law, and if He did so in order to illustrate spiritual truth as well as a correct understanding of Himself, He had a prime opportunity to break a social convention *and* teach the higher law of female leadership in His new order. The question remains, then: Why didn't He do so?

The Staggs face this question (p. 123) by making a subtle suggestion concerning the God-Man Jesus Christ that most evangelicals should find quite disturbing:

The names vary in the four lists, but the male identity is uniform. Why were the Twelve all men? This is the strongest single evidence against a clear breakthrough on the part of Jesus in the recognition of the full equality of women with men. Apostleship was a role distinction, and a primary one in the early church. Why men only? The New Testament gives no clear answer, and there are optional assessments, including the one above, that at this point *even in the example of Jesus there is not a complete overcoming of male bias* [italics mine].

The Staggs suggest that custom concerning women was so "entrenched" that Christ was intimidated and thus chose not to challenge it. The fact that the Lord was not thus inhibited by socio-religious pressures regarding the death penalty is not addressed. Instead, the authors assert that the Lord Himself was restricted by social inhibitions and deficiencies in His own past. They write, "This is not to dismiss the restriction of the Twelve to male Jews as necessarily without male bias. The explanation nearest at hand is that Jesus began where he was, within the structures of Judaism as he knew it in his upbringing." In other words, it is their view that Jesus was as limited by ignorance and an inability to overcome social pressure as was any other man.

The Staggs err further by suggesting that the gender of the Twelve is a moot point. "The logic which from the male composition of the Twelve would exclude women from high office or role in the church would likewise exclude the writers and most of the readers of this book, for there were no non-Jews among the Twelve. Unless one would argue that 'apostolic succession' (however adapted) is for Jews only, it cannot be for men only."

Apparently the authors fail to understand Messiah's prophetic priority of beginning with the house of Israel. They also fail to make a basic distinction presumed in Scripture—that a number of essential differences between apostolic office and function and the administration of God's church in the post-apostolic age exists. As we will see, in fact, it is upon qualifications and restrictions given under apostolic authority that the biblical identification and role of women in the church must ultimately be determined.

## Witnesses of the Resurrection: the Priority of Women in Proclamation of the Resurrection

Without discrimination all persons, male and female, have the honor and duty to proclaim the good news, or gospel, of God's work in Christ. We observed a woman doing this during Christ's ministry. The Samaritan woman brought the testimony of Jesus to the city of Samaria with great results (John 4:28, 39–42).

With the resurrection of Christ there is even greater evidence that women had the same duty of testimony. Certain women in the gospel accounts were instructed to share their testimony of the risen Lord with the apostles and other disciples. Mark 16:1 and Matthew 28:1 and 7 indicate Mary Magdalene, Mary the mother of James, and Salome were so commissioned.

Though the Great Commission in Matthew 28:19–20 was given directly to the apostles, it has generally been viewed as not exclusive to them. Surely among the five hundred who were witnesses of Christ's ascension were many women (1 Cor. 15:6).

## THE ROLE OF WOMEN IN THE MINISTRY OF PAUL

### Paul's Attitude Toward Women

The attitude of Paul toward women was markedly different from that of others trained in rabbinic traditions, both in the social and religious realms. Socially, Paul must be seen as one who recognized the intrinsic worth of woman as equal to that of man. Upon coming to Philippi and finding no synagogue, he quite comfortably preached to a crowd of women (Acts 16:13). The apostle accepted Lydia's invitation to stay at her house apparently without the slightest qualm (Acts 16:15). Whereas in rabbinic custom a woman was mentioned only as the wife of a given man, Paul in the Book of Romans greets women by name. Furthermore, Paul calls Phoebe, who delivered the epistle to the Romans, a sister.

## Women who supported his ministry

Women were very active in the ministry of Paul. They traveled around with him, and many were involved in supporting him financially. Phoebe is called by Paul as a helper to him (Rom. 16:1) and Priscilla is named with her husband as a co-worker (Rom. 16:3). Mary is said to have labored much (Rom. 16:6). Lydia was Paul's first convert in Macedonia and housed Paul and his party in her home (Acts 16:15).

## The fellow-workers of Paul

Women were deeply involved in helping Paul in the ministry. Paul proclaimed the gospel to men and women alike and biblically admonished them alike. The first gospel appeal in Europe was made to the women by the seashore at Philippi. Paul taught Thecla of Iconium while he was in prison. His letters are addressed to men and women both; he refers in 1 Timothy 3:11, for instance, to the work and character of both deacons and deaconesses (or the wives of the deacons). Men and women alike are urged to be sober, patient, and holy (Titus 2:2–8; 1 Tim. 5:1–2). Equally, men and women are condemned for their wickedness (Rom. 1:26-32). Men and women have reciprocal conjugal rights in the marriage, unlike the perspective contemporary to Paul's day.[1]

The New Testament portrays women as valuable to Paul in his ministry, supporting him and laboring with him. At Thessalonica many leading women in the city were attracted to Paul's teaching and, if Joseph Holzner is correct, became the chief support of the church founded by Paul and Silas.[2] The same may be the case at Berea (Acts 17:12). In addition to the financial help of highborn

Greek women, there is the clear statement in Philippians 4:2–3 that two women were co-laborers with Paul in the work of the gospel, though their specific work is unknown. Phoebe is specially commended for her work in the ministry (Rom. 16:1–2). Priscilla, along with her husband, is seen as a fellow worker with the apostle (Rom. 16:3). Additionally, women were commended for their Christian service even though not specifically with Paul (Rom. 16:6, 12, 13, 15).

## Were women fellow-apostles of the apostle?

If *Junia* is the correct reading in Romans 16:7, we may have in this passage a woman called an apostle, one who was a messenger of the church. It may be, however, that Junia merely had a good reputation among the Twelve and Paul, rather than actually being an apostle.

Clark (p. 131) takes the time to delve more fully into this question, which can only be answered by a careful analysis of the text:

> . . . it is grammatically possible that Junia(s) could be a yeoman who is here termed an apostle. On the other hand, it is possible that Junia(s) is a man. In addition, it is even possible that the passage does not identify Andronicus and Junia(s) as apostles at all. The phrase could be translated "they are people well known to the apostles." This translation would mean that the two were among the first Christian converts and known to the Twelve. Hence, it is not clear either that Junia(s) is a woman, or that this person was an apostle. Grammatical considerations leave open the possibility that this passage might refer to a female apostle. However, this possibility has much less weight in view of the evidence that only men were chosen to be apostles and the complete lack of evidence elsewhere for the existence of any female apostle. It is unlikely that this is a reference to a female apostle.

## Did women function as pastors or deaconesses?

One area of lively discussion in this regard is the issue of female leadership in the early centuries of the church through the office of pastor and/or deaconess. If indeed these offices were occupied by women, and if they included the responsibility of expounding the Word of God authoritatively to men as well as to women, then there would seem to exist a direct contradiction to the Pauline prohibitions against women teaching men.

Because of the amount of space needed to address the issue of church offices and women's roles in them, a full discussion will be reserved for a later chapter. Let it suffice here to note that the value of gifted women in ministry was not lost on the New Testament church.

## CONCLUSION

It is obvious that women were highly valued by both Jesus and Paul. Those who argue that women are in any way inferior to men have no foundation in Scripture. Jesus broke with social and religious convention to demonstrate his high regard for women; Paul considered them co-laborers in the task of taking Christ to the world. There is no question that women functioned in important ways in New Testament times.

# The Ministerial Role of Women in the Second and Third Centuries of the Church

## GENERAL ATTITUDE TOWARD WOMEN IN THE CHURCH

The second and third centuries of the Christian era brought with them an evolving church structure, different from that established by the apostles. Changes did not occur at the same rate throughout the empire in which the Christian movement was making its presence known, nor were the fathers of the church unanimous concerning church polity and doctrine. The role of women in the ministry of the church became a practical concern, though it did not attract the same attention given to controversies related to the Person and work of Christ, nor to the doctrinal arguments of the time.

Nevertheless, several documents produced in this two-hundred-year period, as well as the writings of several fathers of the church, include information that provides insight on specific attitudes toward the role of women in the church.[1]

### *"A religion of widows and wives"*

The Christian faith attracted considerable numbers of women in the early years of the church—so much so, in fact, that critics of the movement sardonically claimed it as "a religion of widows and wives."[2] The high estate to which Christianity generally brought women in the an-

79

cient Mediterranean world, in sharp contrast to other phi-
losophies of the time, attracted much criticism. Tatian
(A.D. 110–172), a second-century apologist who wrote a
special treatise to the Greeks in defense of Christianity,
pointed out the statues the Greeks raised to certain morally corrupt women. "And I was willing to speak these
women in order that it might not be regarded by you as
strange when considering what we practice and comparing the statues you see with your eyes, you might not
mock the women who pursue philosophy among us."[3]

Similarly, Clement of Alexandria (A.D. 153–217) spoke
positively of women in a clause reminiscent of Galatians
3:28: "For the one whose life is like ours is, may phi-
losophize without learning, whether barbarian, whether
Greek, whether slave—whether an old man, or a boy, or a
woman."[4] Continuing in the same vein, Clement reflected the essential view of women Paul had revealed in
Galatians, which is also that of Genesis 1:27: "The
woman does not have one human nature, and the man
manifest another, but the same: so also with virtue. If,
then, a self-restraint and righteousness, and whatever
qualities are considered as following them, is the virtue
only of the male, it does belong to the male alone to be
virtuous, and to the woman to be licentious and unrighteous. But it is offensive even to say this."[5]

Likewise, concerning the learning of male and female
and the identification of both as equally man, Clement
was clear:

> For the virtue of man and woman is the same. . . .
> 'For in this world,' he [Jesus] says, 'they marry, and
> are given in marriage,' in which alone the female is
> distinguished from the male; 'but in that world it is
> so no more.' There the rewards of this social and holy
> life, which is based on conjugal union, are laid up,
> not for male and female, but for man, the sexual
> desire which divides humanity being removed.
> Common therefore, too, to men and women, is the
> name of man.[6]

Though Tatian and Clement spoke in reasonably favorable terms about women, there were others among the Fathers who, in their opposition to women occupying offices in the church, became guilty at times of making statements that were biblically unfounded. For example, Epiphanius said that women were easily seduced and lacked wisdom,[7] and Tertullian (A.D. 145–220), often known to be hard in his statements against women, said of them: "Thou art the devil's door."[8]

The author of the Pseudo-Clementine *Homilies* (A.D. 200–250) also presented a low view of women: "And what need is there to say more? The male is wholly truth, the female wholly falsehood. But he who is born of the male and female, in some things speaks truth, in some falsehood. For the female . . . leads the greater part into fornication, and thus deprives them [male and female] of the coming excellent Bridegroom."[9]

Tertullian probably had some of the harshest words for women. At one point he accused all women of being the epitome of Eve:

And do you not know that you are (each) an Eve? The sentence of God on this sex of yours lives in this age: the guilt must of necessity live too. *You* are the devil's gateway: *you* are the unsealer of that (forbidden) tree: *you* are the first deserter of the divine law: *you* are she who persuaded him whom the devil was not valiant enough to attack. *You* destroyed so easily God's image, man. On account of *your* desert—that is, death—even the Son of God had to die.[10]

## PROHIBITIONS AGAINST LEADERSHIP FOR WOMEN

There was considerable agreement among the Fathers (except for those outside the mainstream of orthodoxy) concerning the position of women in the church. Different church leaders at various locations and times allowed service roles for women, but did not allow women to teach and exercise authority over men. In harmony with the Fathers were the various "church orders," a type of literature begun in the Pastorals of the first century.[11]

Tertullian, even after he became a Montanist, spoke often against the participation of women in the worship services. He wrote, referring to the teachings of Paul:

> When prescribing on women silence in the church, that they speak not for the mere purpose of learning [teaching, *discendi*] (though he has already shown that even they have the right to prophesy, when he insists that the woman who prophesies must be covered with a veil), it is from the law that he draws his sanction that woman should be under obedience.[12]

Reference to Paul's teaching in the first letter to the Corinthians and in the Pastorals is not restricted to Tertullian.[13] Origen, as well, relied on the words of the apostle in his instruction to women: "He does not allow woman to teach or lord it over man. He does desire women to be adept at teaching, so as to urge chastity upon young women, not upon young men. It is indeed unbecoming for woman to be a teacher of men. But women should urge young women to be chaste and to love their husbands and children."[14]

Some fragments of other early writings show the same perspective:

> [It is] not, [then, right] either that women be teachers, [especially] concerning the name of the Lord and [His redemp]tive passion. For ye have not been appointed, O women, [in order] to teach, and [especial]ly widows, [but only to importune] God. [For the Teacher himself <when>] He sent us [the twelve] to disciple the Peo[ple and] the Gentiles, *having* along with [us *chosen out*] also [female] dis[ciples]—Mary

[Magdal]ene and M[ary of] James and Salo[me]—He did not send them forth with [us] to disciple *or* <*save*> *the world*. [For if it were] needful that women should [teach], our Teacher [himself] would have bidden these along with us to teach.[15]

One may readily see from the few examples given that in the orthodox community—West, Egypt, and Syria—women were not afforded opportunity to occupy positions of leadership in the church, though the case was entirely different with heretical groups.

## THE FEMININE ROLE IN HERETICAL SECTS

Two major heretical groups stand out concerning the question of women in the ministry: Montanism and Gnosticism.

Many heretical sects during the early centuries of the church paid honor to women, very similar to the honor paid priestesses and vestal virgins by the Greeks and Romans. Nearly every founder of a sect had a woman to assist him. Simon Magnus had Helene, Montanus had Maximilla, and so on.[16] One sect of special notice among the Montanists was known by several names, including Quintiliani, the Pepuziani, and the Priscilliani. In this sect Eve was given recognition for eating first of the tree of knowledge, and Miriam and the daughters of Philip were lauded because they publicly expressed the right of women to prophesy. This sect allowed women to hold the offices of bishops, elders, and deacons, appealing to Paul's word in Galatians 3:28 as support. It may have been because of this group that Tertullian spoke with such zeal against women.[17]

A chief characteristic of Montanism was prophecy. Prophecy was practiced in the Christian church after the turn of the first century,[18] but it began to fall away, often into disrepute. Figures like Montanus, no doubt, helped move it toward that end. Montanus himself claimed to be

the Paraclete of God, and the women with him also
claimed to speak forth prophecies:

> Next to Montanus, yea, soon above him, stood the
> two prophetesses Prisca and Maximilla. Eusebius
> makes report of a Montanistic prophetess named
> Ammia, and Epiphanius mentions a Quintilla.
> Firmilian knows of a Montanistic prophetess in Asia
> Minor who was a cleric, who baptized and who
> administered the Eucharist. Also Didymus reports
> that women taught and prophesied in the
> congregational assemblies of the Montanists.[19]

In his interpretation of 1 Corinthians 14:34–35, Origen, commenting on the question of women teaching, at-
tacked the Montanist prophetesses:

> Although all speak and are allowed to speak when
> they are granted a revelation, 'the women,' he says,
> 'should keep silence in the churches.' They in no way
> fulfill this command, those disciples of women, who
> chose as their master Priscilla and Maximilla, not
> Christ, the Spouse of the Bride. But, let us be good-
> natured players, and cope with the arguments which
> they judge convincing. The Evangelist Philip, they
> say, had four daughters, and all prophesied. If they
> prophesied, what is strange, they ask, if our own
> prophetesses—as they are called—also prophesy? Let
> us then resolve this difficulty. First, since you say:
> 'Our women prophesied,' show in them the signs of
> prophesy. [sic] Second, if the daughters of Philip
> prophesied, at least they did not speak in the
> assemblies; for we do not find this fact in the Acts of
> the Apostles. Much less in the Old Testament. It is
> said that Deborah was a prophetess. Mary, the sister
> of Aaron, tambourine in hand, led the choir of
> women. There is not evidence that Deborah delivered
> speeches to the people, as did Jeremias and Isaias.
> Hulda, who was a prophetess, did not speak to the

people, but only to a man, who consulted her at home. The Gospel itself mentions a prophetess, Anna, the daughter of Phanuel, of the tribe of Aser; but she did not speak publicly. Even if it is granted to a woman to prophesy and show the sign of prophecy, she is nevertheless not permitted to speak in an assembly. When Mary, the prophetess, spoke, she was leading a choir of women. For: 'It is improper for a woman to raise her voice at meetings,' and: 'I am not giving permission for a woman to teach' and even less 'to tell a man what to do.' Although those given above say more categorically that a woman does not have the right by her word to guide a man, I shall further prove this position from another text. 'Bid the old women to behave themselves as befits holy women, teaching what is good, in order to form young women in wisdom,' and not simply 'Let them teach.' Certainly, women should also 'teach what is good,' but men should not sit and listen to a woman, as if there were no man capable of communicating the word of God. 'If they have any question to ask, they should ask their husbands at home: it does not seem right for a woman to raise her voice at meetings.' It seems to me that the expression 'their husbands' does not refer only to husbands; for if that were the case, either virgins would speak in the assembly, or they would have nobody to teach them, and the same is true for widows. And could 'their husbands' not also mean a brother, a relative, or a son? In short, let a woman learn from the man who is her own, 'woman,' 'For it is improper for a woman to speak in an assembly,' no matter what she says, even if she says admirable things, or even saintly things, that is of little consequence, since they come from the mouth of a woman. 'A woman in an assembly': clearly this abuse is denounced as improper—an abuse for which the entire assembly is responsible.[20]

Another major sect of the second and third century was Gnosticism. As in Montanism, the role of women was especially important in Gnosticism, as seen in the place held by women in Gnostic literature. The women of the Gospels, such as Mary, the mother of Jesus, Mary Magdalene, Martha, Salome, and others, received prominent attention.[21]

The Nicolaitans read a work supposedly written by Noria, the assumed wife of Noah. The Naassenes said they received their doctrines from a certain Marianne, who supposedly received them from James, the brother of the Lord. The *Acts of Philip* presented Marianne as the sister of James and showed her as working closely with him. Moreover the *Acts of Paul* associated Thecla with the work of Paul, and named many other prophetesses: Theonoe, Stratonica, Eubulla, Artemilla, Nympha, and Phila.[22]

Without exception, these and other spurious, extracanonical works had little or no basis in history or fact, and proved of little value except as a sourcebook for instituting or confirming dubious traditions in various heretical sects. A good deal of tension existed, therefore, between the mainstream of Christian orthodoxy and the heterodox groups on this very point.

This tension is reflected in a work like *Pistis Sophia* in which Mary Magdalene (representing women's activity) is found in a struggle with Peter (representing the orthodox). One writer describes the scene:

Peter complains that Mary is dominating the conversation with Jesus and displacing the rightful priority of Peter and his brother apostles. He urged Jesus to silence her and is quickly rebuked. Later, however, Mary admits to Jesus that she hardly dares speak to him freely, because, in her words, "Peter makes me hesitate; I am afraid of him, because he hates the female race." Jesus replies that whoever the

Spirit inspires is divinely ordained to speak, whether man or woman.[23]

The various Gnostic branches had women functioning in all positions held only by men in the orthodox church. The Valentian Marcus trained his feminine followers to be prophetesses; they were allowed even to speak the prayers at the celebration of the Lord's supper and to distribute the wine.[24]

Tertullian severely rebuked a prophetess of Marcion whom he had allowed to teach: "These heretical women—how audacious they are! They have no modesty; they are bold enough to teach, to engage in argument, to enact exorcisms, to undertake cures, and, it may be, even to baptize."[25]

The reason for this liberal view of women can possibly be attributed to the Gnostics' androgynous ("man/woman") view of God. Valentinus perceived of God as Mother and Father. Members of this Gnostic group prayed, "From Thee, Father, and through Thee, Mother, the two immortal names, Parents of the divine being, and thou, dweller in heaven, humanity, of the mighty name. . . ."[26]

Elaine Pagels writes,

> Other texts indicate that their authors had wondered to whom a single, masculine God proposed, "Let us make man [adam] in our image, after our likeness" (Genesis 1:26). Since the Genesis account goes on to say that humanity was created "male and female" (1:27), some concluded that the God in whose image we are made must also be both masculine and feminine—both Father and Mother.[27]

Of special interest is the divine Mother, described as the Holy Spirit. The *Apocryphon of John* gives an account of John leaving the scene of the crucifixion with "great grief" and having a vision of the Trinity. He saw the heavens open and a light with three forms. John was addressed with these words: "John, Jo[h]n, why do you doubt, and why are you afraid? . . . I am the one who [is with you (pl.)] for ever. I [am the Father], I am the Mother, I am the Son."[28]

Pagels adds:

> This gnostic description of God—as Father, Mother and Son—may startle us at first, but on reflection, we can recognize it as another version of the Trinity. The Greek terminology for the Trinity, which includes the neuter term for spirit *(pneuma)* virtually requires that the third "Person" of the Trinity be asexual. But the author of the *Secret Book* has in mind the Hebrew term for spirit, *ruah*, a feminine word; and so concludes that the feminine "Person" conjoined with Father and Son must be Mother.[29]

A similar theme is found in the *Gospel of Thomas*, where Jesus contrasted his earthly mother with the true Mother (the Holy Spirit) who gave him life: "And whoever does [not] love his father and his mother as I do cannot become a [disciple] to Me. For My mother [gave My falsehood], but [My] true [Mother] gave Me life."[30]

While this "man/woman" view of God may have greatly contributed to Gnosticism's policy of allowing women in the ministry, three other heretical groups—the Marcionites, the Montanists, and the Carpocratians—viewed God in masculine terms but still allowed women to take positions of leadership.[31] View of God alone, then, did not necessarily dictate a perspective on feminine roles.

The reason these heretical groups allowed women to occupy such roles may have been their rejection of the created order, a rejection found in Gnosticism and possibly extending also to Montanism, as well as to contemporary feminist apologists:

Why is it that especially in Gnosticism the foreground is occupied very much by women and the New Testament directives concerning the 'subjection' of woman are obviously ignored? Our examination of New Testament passages revealed that the command which requires women to be 'in subjection' and to 'keep silence in the churches' is found in creation. This fact, however, is not properly appreciated in Gnosticism. The pronounced dualism in Gnosticism leads in the various gnostic sects either to asceticism or to libertinism, and thus to the dissolution of marriage. The relation of the sexes toward each other, anchored in creation, is leveled in Gnosticism, and this leveling process destroys understanding or appreciation of the Scriptural directive that women be excluded from the public office of teaching in the churches. The relation between creation and redemption was unilaterally dissolved when Gnosticism located the dualism in God Himself and when it declared that the God of creation was the false god of the Jews (Marcion).[32]

## ROLES PRACTICED BY WOMEN IN THE ORTHODOX CHURCH

### The Role of Widows

Widows as a distinct group of women with a particular role in the post-apostolic church are evident in very early church literature. Polycarp was the first to use for them the term "altar of God,"[33] a term appearing often in later church writings. And Ignatius of Antioch referred to the "virgins called widows."[34]

The origin of the order of widows is found in the New Testament, which in turn looks back to Old Testament precepts. Widows in ancient Israel were very vulnerable. In view of this, special provisions were made for them in Israelite law (Ex. 22:21ff; Deut. 14:29; 16:11, 14; 24:17).

The prophets had especially harsh words for those who were unjust toward widows (Isa. 1:23; 10:2; Ps. 94:6; Mal. 3:5). Since they were susceptible to mistreatment, God had special concern for them (Ps. 68:5; 146:9; Prov. 15:25), and one's attitude toward widows was a mark of true religion (Job 29:13; Isa. 1:17).

The Christian church inherited this conscience concerning widows. James, clearly reflecting the Old Testament perspective, said that to minister to the widow and orphan in their distress is a true and unambiguous mark of religion (James 1:27). This ideological concern became a practical one in the case of the Greek widows who were failing to receive their proper share in the distribution of food. Seven men, full of the Holy Spirit and wisdom, were given charge over them (Acts 6:1–4). (Some have attempted to find in this passage the establishment of the office of deacons and the order of widows, but probably neither is intended here.)

The apostle Paul instructed widows that it was good for them to marry again, though this was not a command (1 Cor. 7:8, 9, 39). He advised young widows in Ephesus to marry again lest they be overcome by the desires of the flesh (1 Tim. 5:11).

A major passage relating to the role of widows is 1 Timothy 5:3–16. In these verses three classes of godly widows are discussed.[35]

The first group were those women whose husbands had died but whose family—children and other relatives—were instructed to take care of them (5:4, 8, 16).[36]

The second class of widows had no family for support and were in financial need. These were called the true or real widows. They gave themselves to "supplications and prayers" (5:3, 5, 16).

The last group were the "enrolled widows."[37] Everett Ferguson says of this class, "To put it in the language of today, she has been put on the payroll of the church. She becomes a paid servant of the church. She is a represen-

tative of the church, supported to perform services on behalf of the church."[38]

One should *not* understand, then, two classes of godly
widows: those supported by their family and those over
sixty supported by the church. Would the church refuse
aid to widows under sixty who had no one else to meet
their need? Hardly! All those godly women who did not
have children or other family and needed help were supported. But a few from the larger group [39] were registered
for special work because of their testimony and ability.

The enrolled widow was described as follows: 1) She
was at least sixty years old; 2) she must have led a pure
married life; 3) she had a reputation for good works, having a) reared children; b) showed hospitality; c) washed
the saints' feet (probably literally and figuratively);
d) helped those in trouble; e) followed every kind of good
work.[40]

The listing of qualifications for these widows is similar
to that for the overseers, deacons, and deaconesses in
1 Timothy 3:1–13 and Titus 3:6–9. One writer says that
the standards for the widows are not arbitrary but are a
"pointer to her ministry."[41]

The standards concerning age and purity of life would
have helped avoid problems with younger widows who
might marry again or get into trouble as they went from
house to house ministering to others (1 Tim. 5:11–15).
Likewise, past good works would indicate the dedication
of one to be registered by the church for its ministry.

It is very important to notice that enrollment itself dis-
tinguished one group of widows from widows in general
and established an order parallel to other orders in the
church. It was with this special group of widows that
the post-apostolic writers concerned themselves, though
the former type of widow was not entirely forgotten in the
early church.[42]

The *Apostolic Church Order*, known also as *Third
Clement*,[43] listed the responsibilities of the widows as

prayer and ministry to women who were sick: "Two to devote themselves to prayer on behalf of all who are tempted, and to revelations to whatever extent is necessary, one to succour women who are sick. They must be ready to help, they must be temperate and make the necessary reports to the priest."[44]

The duties of the widows, other than praying, teaching women, doing good deeds, and possibly being involved in some way in the liturgy, were restricted. They were not to answer questions of a theological nature, but rather to refer these to the leaders of the community. Were she to do otherwise, the Word of God would be mocked rather than praised by unbelievers:

> It is neither right nor necessary therefore that women should be teachers, and especially concerning the name of Christ and the redemption of His passion. For you have not been appointed to this, O women, and especially widows, that you should teach, but that you should pray and entreat the Lord God. For He, the Lord God, Jesus Christ our Teacher, sent us the Twelve to instruct the people and the Gentiles; and there were with us women disciples, Mary Magdalene and Mary the daughter of James and the other Mary; but He did not send them to instruct the people with us. For if it were required that women should teach, our Master Himself would have commanded these to give instruction with us.[45]

In similar vein the *Didascalia* prohibited a woman to baptize: "For if it were lawful to be baptized by a woman, our Lord and Teacher Himself would have been baptized by Mary His mother, whereas He was baptized by John. . . . Do not therefore imperil yourselves, brethren and sisters, by acting beside the law of the Gospel."[46]

It is apparent, then, that the question of office and ordination arose with respect to widows. Were they clergy or laity? The terminology used by the Fathers and the variety of practices in the West, Egypt, and Syria make this a difficult question to answer.

The *Apostolic Tradition* says that some widows were appointed but not ordained.[47] Another prominent figure of the West, Tertullian, recognized an order of widows and seemed to reckon them among the clergy. They were subject to similar qualifications regarding marriage and purity, but were forbidden the right to teach or perform a sacramental act. Their high place was recognized in the practice of sinners prostrating themselves in the center of the assembly before the widows and the presbyters.[48]

There can be little question that the Alexandrian fathers listed widows right alongside the bishops, presbyters, and deacons. Clement declared: "Innumerable commands such as these are written in the Holy Bible appertaining to chosen persons, some to presbyters, some to bishops, some to deacons, others to widows. . . ."[49] Origen wrote similarly, "Not only fornication but also second marriages shut off access to ecclesiastical dignities: neither the bishop, nor the presbyter, nor the deacon, nor the widow may be married twice."[50]

A very important distinction, however, was maintained. Most significantly, when a widow was appointed, she was not ordained, as were the bishop, the presbyter, and the deacon. Ordination involved a laying on of hands accompanied by prayer. In the case of the widow, however, there was nothing similar; she was simply named. Ordination was conferred on members of the clergy who played a role in liturgical services,[51] in which widows, for the most part, were not involved.

The order of widows, or the appointed widows, had as their primary duty continence and prayer. Younger widows, even though they could not be established (appointed), were to work toward the same ideal.[52] Thus only the Western church had any ranking of women with the clergy, and even there a distinction was carefully made.

In none of the orthodox centers of the Christian church do we find widows functioning in male roles. Even Tertullian and Hippolytus do not reveal any ministerial position. The order of widows had disappeared entirely by the time of Cyprian, and at Rome it apparently did not exist at the beginning of the third century. Chrysostom attested the position of widow up to the end of the fourth century, but by the middle of the second century it had begun a decline. A major reason for its demise was the rise of asceticism and the emphasis on virginity, constituting an ideal of perfection to which the widows could not attain because of their formerly "defiled" state of marriage.[53]

## The Role of Virgins

Questions about the role of virgins arose in the time of Paul when the Corinthians, influenced by an incipient Gnosticism, appealed to him to settle their differences on virginity, marriage, second marriage, and widowhood. Paul presented a clear teaching that marriage was honorable and not to be despised.[54]

But even with this clear teaching in Scripture, some church fathers taught unorthodox views on marriage. Justin, Athenagoras, and Clement of Alexandria maintained a view of marriage similar to advocates of Stoicism that the sole purpose of marriage was for the continuance of the race.[55]

Though the second and third centuries brought a preoccupation with the glories of martyrdom, Christian asceticism (self-denial, especially in relation to physical comfort) ran a close second. Part of the value of virginity and the self-control it required, so it was thought, was that it was a state of "perfection" that prepared one for martyrdom. The high ideal of virginity and its accompanying asceticism is found in an alleged sermon of Paul in the *Acts of Paul and Thecla*, in which Paul supposedly spoke about self-control and the resurrection:

*Blessed are the pure in heart*
  *for they shall see God.*

*Blessed are they that have kept the flesh chaste*
*for they shall become a temple of God.*
*Blessed are they that control themselves*
*for God shall speak with them.*
*Blessed are they that have kept aloof from this world*
*for they shall be called upright.*
*Blessed are they that have wives as not having them*
*for they shall receive God for their portion.*
*Blessed are they that have the fear of God*
*for they shall become angels of God.*
*Blessed are they that have kept the baptism*
*for they shall rest beside the Father and the Son.*
*Blessed are the merciful*
*for they shall obtain mercy and shall not see the*
*bitter day of judgment.*
*Blessed are the bodies of virgins*
*for they shall be well pleasing to God, and shall*
*not lose the reward of their chastity.*[56]

Evidently the author interpreted the apostle's biblical
teaching about self-control as a reference to a purity different from the actual idea. Thus Howe observes that "the
word . . . is used to denote celibacy or virginity rather
than abstention from unlawful sexual activity. Such an
interpretation indicates that the presbyter was influenced
by the same encratite modes of thought which were current in the Ebionite, Gnostic and Montanist movements
of the time."[57]

Little evidence exists for the ministry of virgins in a
particular role in the second century. Apparently they
were not an order at that time. Toward the middle of the
third century, however, an order of virgins could be found
in all the churches of the East, evidently because circumstances warranted such a role. Widowhood began to fall
into disrepute and virginity became the ideal. Widowhood
evidenced a certain lack of self-control and purity which
lessened one's fitness for service in the church in this period of asceticism.

Virgins began to be appointed to the functions of widows, to the point that Tertullian disapprovingly spoke of a virgin called a widow who, at less than twenty years of age, had been placed in the order of the widows. Tertullian considered such a practice totally unacceptable, and believed that Paul's instruction (that a widow be sixty years of age, married, a mother, and someone who had taught her own children) had been disregarded.[58]

Tertullian did not seem to accept any particular role for virgins but recognized the proper function of the church toward widows, and certainly did not see how a virgin ever could be a widow. Yet, in his letter to the Smyrneans, Ignatius of Antioch wrote, "Greeting to the families of my brothers, along with their wives and children, and to the virgins called widows."[59]

One wonders why the Christian community of Smyrna gave the title of widow to a virgin. Some have thought the term was used because they did the same work as the order of widows.[60] Roger Gryson discounts this and offers his view:

> The point is that in First Timothy the widows recognized and "registered" as such professed continence; in fact, since young widows might want to remarry later on and thus break their "first pledge," *(proten pistin)*, they were refused registration. Consequently, Christian virgins who resolved to remain chaste "for the honor of the Lord's flesh" were called "widows"; since both groups of women had a profession of continence as their chief characteristic, their ideals and life-styles seemed similar.[61]

## The Role of Deaconesses

The role of deaconesses began to gain prominence as that of the widows declined partly because the role of deaconesses was largely practiced by virgins whose chaste and ascetic state became the ideal, and partly because deaconesses took over many of the tasks of the widows.[62]

The office of deaconess was already a position for women in the service of the Christian community in apostolic times, but it was an inferior office until the middle of the third century. The office was evident at the beginning of the second century when Pliny wrote to Trajan (ca. A.D. 112) about Christians in Bithynia, "I have judged it necessary to obtain information by torture from two female slaves whom they call 'deaconesses',"[63] the latter term in Latin probably a translation of the Greek *diakonos*.[64]

The office of both widow and deaconess appear to represent a gradual development.[65] But the function of the deaconess was not greatly expanded from that of the widow. She had the primary duties of ministering to women in their houses and assisting at baptisms:

> Wherefore, O bishop, appoint thee workers of righteousness as helpers who may cooperate with thee unto salvation. Those that please thee out of all the people thou shalt choose and appoint as deacons, a man for the performance of most things that are required, but a woman for the ministry of women. For there are houses whither thou canst not send a deacon to the women, on account of the heathen, but mayest send a deaconess. Also, because in many other matters the office of a woman deacon is required. In the first place, when women go down into the water, those who go down into the water ought to be anointed by a deaconess with the oil of anointing; and where there is no woman at hand, and especially a deaconess, it is not fitting that women should be seen by men [early baptisms were done with the person unclothed]: but with the imposition of hand do thou anoint the head only. As of old the priests and kings were anointed in Israel, do thou in like manner, with the imposition of hand, anoint the head of those who receive baptism, whether of men or of women; and afterwards—whether thou thyself baptize, or thou command the deacons or presbyters

to baptize—let a woman deacon, as we have already said, anoint the women.

But let a man pronounce over them the invocation of the divine Names in the water. And when she who is being baptized has come up from the water, let the deaconess receive her, and teach and instruct her how the seal of baptism ought to be (kept) unbroken in purity and holiness. For this cause we say that the ministry of a woman deacon is especially needful and important. For our Lord and Savior also was ministered unto by women ministers, Mary Magdalene, and Mary the daughter of James and mother of Jose. . . . And thou also has need of the ministry of a deaconess for many things; for a deaconess is required to go into the houses of the heathen where there are believing women, and to visit those who are sick, and to minister to them in that of which they have need, and to bathe those who have begun to recover from sickness.[66]

Later, by the late fourth century A.D., the deaconess received additional responsibilities of "assigning places to female strangers, of keeping order, and of admonishing and praying with latecomers," as well as assisting in a minor way at the altar.[67] But even in the eastern empire, where opportunities for women were often greater, her duties and rights were limited. "The right to anoint the head and to perform the baptismal act itself is reserved, also when women are being served, for the deacon or presbyter. Where cleric activity begins, there the competence of the deaconess ends."[68]

Clement and Origen spoke of deaconesses in the ministry of the early church, and especially those associated with Paul, but gave no indication that the office survived that period, let alone that it survived in Egypt in their own time. When they spoke of ministries, they made no mention of deaconesses.

The western church gives us even less information about deaconesses than the Egyptian: "Tertullian, like all the West up to the end of the fourth century, ignored completely the institution of deaconesses."[69]

Even as events and attitudes caused deaconesses to supplant the widows of the eastern church, so time brought the demise of the order of deaconesses. Only the eastern church had made much of the office at all in the first two post-apostolic centuries, and though it existed for a time after that, with even the western church adopting it for a short while, the order had vanished in the West by the eighth century and in the East[70] by the tenth. It is still, however, preserved in some senses in the Greek Orthodox Church.[71]

The reasons for the ultimate demise of the office of deaconess may have been the decline in missionary activity of the church and in the baptisms with which deaconesses assisted; the reaction against the prominent ministry of women in certain heretical groups; and the rise of religious orders which absorbed and redirected the activities of deaconesses.[72]

## CONCLUSION

We can easily see that little progress was made from the time of the New Testament into the second and third centuries for teaching or leadership roles of women over men in the church. None of the fathers or the writers who documented early church history (except those from heterodox sects) reveal a sanction for women to serve as teachers of men, elders, or in other typically male functions.

Women did, however, have important ministerial roles as widows and deaconesses. In these positions they assisted men in caring for the needs of women. So then, classes of women servants of the church which already existed in the New Testament in embryonic form were allowed to expand and be better defined. But women, in agreement with New Testament teaching, were not allowed to have authority over men in the church.

## CHAPTER SIX

# Are Men and Women Equal?
# Separating Essence from Function

## THE IMPORTANCE OF GALATIANS
## 3:28 TO THE QUESTION

"There is neither Jew nor Greek . . . slave nor free . . .
male nor female; for you are all one in Christ Jesus" (Gal.
3:28). Those who advocate female leadership in the
church today use this passage as a classic proof text. Since
it has such importance to feminists in their arguments[1]
for the leadership of women in teaching, preaching, and
holding traditional male roles, we need to look at these
arguments carefully in its light.

### Is Galatians 3:28 the "acid test"?

Feminists consider Galatians 3:28 one of the most important passages in the entire New Testament concerning
the functional equality of all persons in Christ. Paul Jewett calls Galatians 3:28 "the Magna Carta of Humanity,"[2]
and the last word on the subject; Christ could say no
more.[3] Such statements may sound wonderful, but they
are woefully difficult to prove. In fact, Galatians 3:28 does
not at all argue that women are functionally interchangeable with men in the Christian community.

Paul's teaching in this passage is apparently the *tour de
force* to feminists Letha Scanzoni and Nancy Hardesty. In
what appears to be a statement of a canon within the
canon, they write in *All We're Meant to Be* (p. 71), as
noted earlier, "Of all the passages concerning women in

100

the New Testament, only Galatians 3:28 is in a doctrinal setting; the remainder are all concerned with practical matters."

But not all feminist scholars share the euphoric understanding of Galatians 3:28 that Scanzoni and Hardesty espouse. Madeleine Boucher, in "Some Unexplored Parallels" (pp. 50-60) describes the significance of Galatians 3:28 in less optimistic terms:

> What Gal. 3:28 is saying is that persons of both high and low position can be brought together in the Church. If so, then Paul was not calling for any social reforms; inequalities would continue to exist in the Church. Paul fully intended that women and slaves remain in the subordinate place in which he thought God had put them. The only practical change demanded by Paul—and this is the thrust of Gal. 3:28—was the admission of Gentiles, law-free, into the Church. He was saying: if the admittedly inferior slave and woman had a place in the Church (as in the Synagogue) why not also the Gentile? This might be described more accurately as a baptismal-ecclesiological statement than as a theological statement directed against the order of creation. In any case, Gal. 3:28, as much as the first two texts, seems to assume a dichotomy between the social order and life *coram Deo*.

While I do not agree with Boucher's negativism about Paul's position on slaves and women, I do agree that Paul is not speaking to social issues or ramifications in his statement of oneness in Christ. Instead, as subsequent exegesis will demonstrate, Paul is teaching here that no areas of discrimination exist in reference to heirship in the Abrahamic covenant to all those who have faith in Christ. He further clarifies that point by referring to the unity of all believers, all those who are baptized into Christ.

## What Does "Neither Male nor Female" Mean?

What is the meaning and application of Galatians 3:28 to those who argue for interchangeability of roles for male and female in the church?

Feminists believe the phrase "neither male nor female" obliterates all role distinctions between male and female in the Christian community.[4] One leading voice for elimination of role distinction argues that the apostle presented two points in this passage: (1) He was reversing the order of creation, establishing the new redemptive order; (2) The Jew/Gentile, slave/free, and male/female categories are functional, rather than merely positional. Stendahl writes, "Just as Jews and Greeks remained what they were, so man and woman remain what they are; but in Christ, by baptism and hence in the church—not only in faith—something has happened which transcends the Law itself and thereby even the order of creation."[5]

Robin Scroggs, in "Women in the NT" (The Interpreter's Dictionary of the Bible, p. 966), also believes the passage demonstrates the obliteration of role distinctions between male and female. He writes, "To enter the Christian community thus meant to join a society in which male-female roles and valuations based on such roles had been discarded. The community was powerless to alter role valuations in the outside culture, but within the church, behavior and interrelationships were to be based on this affirmation of equality."

The faculty of Christ Seminary (Seminex), in a study document on the ordination of women, maintain that the passage is not to be restricted simply to the spiritual or heavenly sphere but is to be applied in a concrete and physical way in the present. To do otherwise is to pervert the gospel. Such concrete and physical application means, to these scholars, the ordination of women, which they see as the logical and theological conclusion of Galatians 3:28 and, indeed, of the gospel itself.

But to truly understand the point Paul was making in

this passage, we must recognize that the Galatians text finds its authority in Genesis 1:26–28, especially verse 27: "Male and female He created them." The Genesis text concerns the very being and nature of male and female, and since both were made in the image of God, Paul could use this text to best emphasize the unity of male and female as new creations in Christ.

## HOW THE CREATION NARRATIVES ARE USED BY THE APOSTLE PAUL

Paul developed his teaching on appropriate authority roles for women from the creation and fall narratives of Genesis 1–3. These teachings are recorded in Galatians 3:26–28; 1 Corinthians 11:7–12; 1 Timothy 2:11–15; and 1 Corinthians 14:34 (if one considers the "law" in this last verse to be a reference to Genesis 3:16b).

Genesis 1:26–28 concerns the essential created nature of male and female. Both were made in God's image. Stylistically verse 27 is a synonymous parallelism, with the first part of verse 27 emphasizing man as the *creation of God*, the second part stressing man as created in the *divine image*, and the third part portraying man—who is in God's image—as created *male and female*. In addition, each of the key phrases (italicized here) is stressed in the text by its occurrence at the first of each phrase.[6]

This verse obviously teaches that male and female are the creation of God and bear the divine image. In the words of Walther Eichrodt, "Because man and woman emerge at the same time from the hand of the Creator, and are created in the same way after God's image, the difference between the sexes is no longer relevant to their position before God."[7]

Paul, in harmony with Moses, the author of Genesis, could emphasize in Galatians 3:28 the unity of male and female as created in the image of God while at the same time maintaining the distinction of the sexes.

## THE DIFFERENCES AND SIMILARITIES
## BETWEEN MALE AND FEMALE

No matter how ardently feminists, both secular and evangelical, deny the existence of essential differences between the sexes, it is nevertheless true that such differences do exist and have been acknowledged by every known society in recorded history. As Stephen Clark notes (p. 371):

> Many of these differences, such as muscular strength, vocal pitch, sexual function, and anatomy, are plainly visible to all peoples. However, most societies place much weight on other types of differences between men and women—differences in personality, social relating, and aptitude. If differences such as these exist between men and women, as most societies assume, then the belief that men's and women's roles should be structured in an identical fashion receives important support. For this reason, debate over the existence, extent, and significance of the differences between men and women has been a prominent feature of the current controversy concerning men's and women's roles.

Clark then pursues a more detailed examination of scientific as well as social evidence supporting essential differences between men and women, striving all the while for comparisons that are descriptive without being evaluative. He is also careful to point out that no such distinctions are absolute, and that both sexes possess to some degree all the traits in question.

What is the point of arguing the obvious, that essential differences do exist between women and men? If Paul argues the point of Galatians 3:28 or any other passage based on created order, it behooves us to understand the process as well as the product of creation if we are to properly understand the application of the passage as a proof text.

## WHAT PAUL WAS TEACHING
## IN GALATIANS 3:28

### Equal Heirs

The verses immediately preceding Galatians 3:28 discuss the nature of justification and how a person may be included in the Abrahamic covenant. Paul insisted that entrance into the covenant is by faith (v. 22), not works.[8] Just as sin is the greater equalizer and all are prisoners of sin (v. 23), so faith also is an equalizer, and all believers—Jew and Gentile, slave and free, male and female—are by faith included in the Abrahamic covenant and promise. Paul's use of "sons of God"in verse 26 for all the indicated pairs is especially instructive; because both women and men are included in the term, it obviously extends beyond a purely physical dimension.

The use of "son" should not confuse us, since the masculine pronoun for the Christian is used throughout Galatians (1:11; 3:15; 4:12; 5:11, 13; 6:1, 18). Apparently Paul used the term "son" as synonomous with "heir" (see Gal. 4:7, 31). Therefore, in Galatians 3:26–28, Paul was saying that no kind[9] of person who has faith in Jesus Christ is excluded from the *position* of being a child of Abraham.

Does this equality in heirship demand equality in *role* or *function* in the church? Feminist evangelicals believe so. Scroggs writes, for instance: "To enter the Christian community thus meant to join a society in which male-female roles and valuations based on such roles had been discarded. The community was powerless to alter role valuations in the outside culture, but within the church, behavior and inter-relationships were to be based on this affirmation of equality."[10]

The apostle's emphasis in the passage, however, is not on social equality between the pairs, but on unity in the one man.[11] An interpretation of Galatians 3:28 which advocates interchangeability of roles between males and females in the church[12] is totally foreign to the meaning and intention of the apostle Paul. Paul's statement in Galatians 3:28 refers only to the *position* one has through faith in Christ, as evidenced by the terms "sons of God," "Abraham's seed," and "heirs according to the promise." These statements clearly and consistently demonstrate Paul's intended meaning.

Any conclusions about this text should reflect Paul's concern with the believer's entrance into the Abrahamic covenant. We cannot draw implications of *function* in society and church from a context concerned with one's *position* as an heir, by faith, of the promises to Abraham. The other pairs in verse 28 (Jew and Greek, slave and free) are in the same category. Any conclusions about the roles of Gentiles in the church or about freedom from slavery, therefore, should not be derived from this verse, but rather supported by other passages that specifically discuss these issues.

To be sure, the provisions of the Abrahamic covenant may extend far beyond the pairs specifically mentioned by Paul, but they must be in harmony with his intentions. Whether one is a child or an adult, rich or poor, black or white, he or she has equal access by faith to the Abrahamic covenant—equal position in Christ. The factors of age, wealth, or color are immaterial to the inheritance since the position is based on faith, not on physical or social considerations. But we cannot violate the meaning of the text by drawing illogical conclusions, such as the determination that since everyone in society has equal access by faith to the covenant promises, order, authority, and variation of roles in Christian society should not exist. Or that since male and female are both equally "sons" of God, they should have interchangeable roles. This is *non sequitur* reasoning.

Paul is not addressing a question of roles for any group. That is not his concern; one's position before God is his concern. He does not argue for or against roles at all; rather, he contrasts faith by the promise with works by the Law.

Paul's teaching on the equality of all people of faith in their inclusion in God's covenant promises and as heirs to the grace of God is also presented in Romans 2:11, where he says there is no human preference with God, and in Romans 10:13, where he claims that everyone who calls on the Lord's name will be saved. The question of role distinction and function, as can be demonstrated by comparing Paul's other letters addressing the subject of women in the church is simply not the issue in Galatians 3.

## CONCLUSION

Paul's teaching on the unity of male and female in the person of the one Man, Christ, is a pivotal doctrine for the church. His focus on unity in Christ for all people, however, has been of secondary importance for those feminists who use the Scripture in Galatians 3:28 to argue for interchangeability of roles between men and women in society and in the church. But their view on this text just does not accord with the evidence.

Paul does quote from Genesis 1:27 that there is neither male nor female, and he most assuredly believes male and female to be image bearers equally. This does not mean, however, that Paul believed the distinctive roles established in creation (Genesis 2) are to be done away with. Rather, Paul considered the sharing of the divine image to be that spark lost in the Fall—the spark renewed in Christ Jesus. Surely the order of creation is passing away, and we are sharing in the eschaton or last days. But *both* are in force and in different ways.

Stretching Galatians 3:26–28 to teach otherwise violates the Scripture and demeans God's work in creation and redemption.

## CHAPTER SEVEN

# May Women Preach or Pray in Church?

Let's return for a moment to the woman who wanted to have a pulpit ministry once every four Sundays. Already she has argued that since women in the New Testament fulfilled prophetic ministry, the way is cleared for her to proclaim the Word of God from the pulpit to a mixed audience. Moreover, she has on many occasions offered prayer from the pulpit and has read the morning Scripture passage. She wants to know how in the world delivering a message can be any different from these duties.

Through a careful examination of 1 Corinthians 11 as well as 1 Timothy 2, we will see that a great deal of difference exists between the various activities associated with the receiving of revelation during the apostolic age, personal worship for the individual believer, and corporate worship for the church of Jesus Christ.

We will see, also, that while Paul's teaching definitely assented that women may exercise a Spirit-controlled gift of prophecy, it nevertheless also indicated that women may not exercise the duty of authoritative proclamation of written revelation (preaching) before a mixed audience. The exercise of prophecy during the apostolic age was not an exercise of headship, as is the proclamation of authoritative revelation today. In other words, prophecy does not equal preaching. As for public prayer, our study will show that the Scriptures do allow women to pray in public, as indicated by the connection of prayer with prophecy in 1 Corinthians 11, and by the argument of 1 Timothy 2.

108

In 1 Corinthans 11:2–16, Paul offered an interesting, though sometimes perplexing, discussion of women praying and prophesying. The circumstances under which these activities took place have been a problem for some interpreters, and several other problems arise when we seek to examine the passage—obscure problems such as the wearing of headcoverings and the presence of angels at congregational worship.[1]

But other less problematic issues are more directly related to our present topic: specifically, the role of apostolic tradition in the understanding of the passage; the significance of the real-life context; the meaning of the Greek word for *head*; the role of the second creation narrative as a basis for Paul's teaching; and the impact of Paul's thinking about the Christian church on the Corinthian church itself.

## THE NATURE OF BIBLICAL HEADSHIP

### The Setting

The apostle began 1 Corinthans 11 immediately after a discussion about the improper ways the Corinthians had taken advantage of their freedom in Christ. Possibly picking up their phrase, "All things are lawful," he reminded them that though all things are indeed lawful, not all are necessary, nor do they always edify (10:23). He had given them several gentle rebukes throughout the letter (1:10–11; 3:1ff; 4:7–13, 18; 5:1–3; 6:1–8; 7:1–5; 8:9–12; 10:1–14). Then in chapter 10 he began a section of praise for their remembrance of him and their adherence to the traditions he had delivered to them. Following that, he proceeded to correct a specific problem concerning the abuse of freedom in Christ by some women in the Corinthian assembly. The context of Paul's correction was that of public worship, which is a point upon which a majority of commentators and authors agree.

## The Instruction

Having praised the Corinthians, then, on their positive response to apostolic tradition thus far, he introduced further instruction that apparently he had not yet given them. The new tradition probably was not merely that the husband occupies a position of authority over the wife—this teaching was already evident in the Old Testament and practiced (and often overpracticed!) in society—but that the position of authority is inherent in the divine order: Christ is over every man; man is over woman; God is over Christ.

It is important to recognize that the discussion was obviously not in reference to the *essence* of the pairs mentioned, since God was said to be the "head" of Christ, who is co-equal with God the Father. The passage refers instead to *function*.[2]

## The Structure of 1 Corinthians 11:3

Paul's placement of the three clauses and the order of the subjects within the clauses, namely, man/Christ; woman/man; Christ/God, is difficult to understand. In a discussion of the order of authority, we would expect Paul to arrange the clauses with each authority listed first, paired with the one over whom authority was exercised, and then placed in descending order (God, Christ, man, woman). But on closer examination, such a hierarchical view of the passage is not required since the couplets are not necessarily logically related in Paul's line of thinking.

For example, there is no need to equate the "every man" of verse 3a with the "man" of verse 3b; the first "man" is more inclusive than the second. It has no limits and includes all men (probably believers, in Paul's thinking). On the contrary, the "man" of verse 3b relates specifically to man in respect to his relationship with woman. Even though there is no logical *progression* of units, it would be a mistake not to see the overall argument as a proof of hierarchical authority based on similar arrangements or like models. The structure here might be called an *inclusio*, very similar to the type of structure found in Genesis 1:26–28 where verse 27 is the focus of the passage. In other words, Paul surrounds the main theme, the headship of man, with the headships of Christ and God. This view might be graphed as follows:

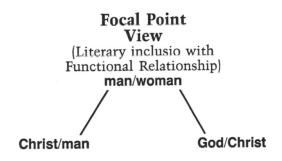

**Focal Point
View**
(Literary inclusio with
Functional Relationship)
**man/woman**

**Christ/man**          **God/Christ**

### *The Meaning of* Head

The pinnacle of verse 3 is the word *head* (*kephale* in Greek). The verse revolves around how God, Christ, and man are "the head."[3] The meaning of this word in Paul's writings (especially here and in Ephesians 5) has been a matter of much dispute. But, as analyzed in Chapter 2, *head* refers to authority rather than "origin" or "source" as some feminists have contended.

The general meaning of a word, as pointed out earlier in our discussion, is known as the "normal" or "natural" meaning. It is a general meaning because it is the most common use of the term. This general meaning is also known as the "unmarked" meaning; in other words, it is the meaning we would assume apart from a literary context that points to a meaning other than the general meaning.[4]

To review, the common or unmarked meaning of *kep-*

*hale* is the physical head. From that meaning come other meanings, such as capital punishment (losing one's head), the prominent part of something (as the head is to the body), or the ruler of something to someone (as the head is of the body).

### The Significance of Headship

But what is the purpose of the instruction in verse 3 in light of the overall passage? Quite simply, the various headships cited by Paul provide the theological foundation for the remainder of the apostle's instruction. In other words, the key to a proper role relationship between man and woman is to recognize that Christ has headship over man[5] in the same way that man has headship over woman.

Even a brief look at the following verses indicates that the headship of man over woman is the focus of the passage. The apostle uses *head* as the central concept in his argument, and around it revolves the reason for the submissiveness of the woman who prophesies or prays. When she expresses her charismatic function within the church, she is to recognize that redemption does not release her from the order of creation. Even as Christ has a head, God—so the woman has a head, man.[6] She is to take that knowledge into account when she prophesies, lest she dishonor man (her head and the source of her being in creation) and her own dignity.

## IS PROPHESYING THE SAME AS PREACHING?

### The Nature of Prophecy

If women were allowed to prophesy in the Corinthian church (and probably this is the proper understanding of the text),[7] the nature of this activity must be understood.

In the Old Testament, only four women were mentioned as being prophetesses: Miriam (Ex. 14:20), Deborah (Judg. 4:4), Huldah (2 Kings 22:14), and Noadiah (Neh. 6:14).[8] With the coming of the Spirit of Pentecost, more women appeared to have access to the prophetic office (Acts 2:17–18).[9] At Corinth this seems to have been the situation; there can be little question that women prophesied there alongside men.[10] But what exactly did prophecy entail, and what, if any, distinction was made between men and women in that ministry?

The text indicates there were actually two activities, praying and prophesying, and both were an effect of the Spirit's operation (1 Cor. 12:10–11). Though the Greek text allows for concepts paired in this way to be either in sharp contrast to each other or closely related, probably the latter use is the one seen here. Prayer and prophecy were equally typical of the prophet's activity in the Old Testament (note Abraham in Gen. 20:7; Samuel in 1 Sam. 12:23; and Jeremiah in Jer. 27:18). Examples of this combination of prayer and prophecy also are found in the New Testament (Anna the prophetess, Luke. 2:27).

Based on these observations, it is clear that neither prophesying nor praying were equated with teaching in the Old Testament or in the New Testament church. Daniélou rightly observes:

> One thing is certain, women are not allowed to teach in the Christian congregation. Perhaps this was something which had actually taken place, which explains why S. Paul forbids it. Yet it seems to have been altogether and always excluded. It is expressly this preaching of the Word to the congregation that is indicated by [lalein], a high-flown style of word which emphasizes the sacred and liturgical character of the preaching (cf. Hebrews 13:7). . . . But the role of the prophet in the Church is not primarily that of giving instruction: this is the duty of the teacher. The prophetic role is essentially concerned with prayer. If we look again at the text from 1 Corinthians we notice that it speaks of "every man or every woman who prays . . . or prophesies." Even if the giving of instruction is thus forbidden to women, it does not

seem that they would be prevented from praying aloud in church.[11]

Though a prophetess might pray and give inspired utterance, she apparently was restricted from the office of teaching in the early church congregation.[12] In fact, there appears to be no such function either in the Old Testament or early Judaism.

At this point, we should consider the arguments of a group of scholars who believe that women, according to 1 Corinthians 11:2–16 and 1 Timothy 2:8–15, may serve as preachers or teachers over men in the public life of the church, as long as they do not usurp authority over the men in the church. One such expositor has contended that prophecy and preaching are synonymous:

> It is safe to conclude that "prophecy" and "preaching" are really synonymous. . . . In most cases, prophesying simply represents the activity of receiving God's message and passing it on. Before the time the written revelation was complete, the prophet received his message directly from God. Once the writers had inscripturated God's message, however, the preacher as God's spokesman, took it from the printed page and heralded it far and wide.[13]

Equating prophecy and preaching may serve as justification for women being allowed to teach men and preach to the Christian assembly—but such a perspective on the nature of prophecy appears contrary to the meaning of the word. One scholar, Oscar Cullman, correctly distinguishes between prophecy and preaching. He points out that preaching and teaching are founded on an intelligible exposition of the Word of God, whereas prophecy is based on direct revelation.[14] This is in agreement with Harold Hoehner's observations concerning "prophesy" and "prophecy":

In the New Testament the verb form . . . is used
twenty-eight times and it always has (with the
possible exception of John 11:51) the idea of
revelation flowing from God. Paul uses it eleven
times. He uses it nine times in 1 Corinthians 12–14
and two times in 1 Corinthians 14 [4–5]. The noun
. . . is used nineteen times in the New Testament.
Paul uses it once in Romans 12:6 and five times in
1 Corinthians 12–14. The consistent New Testament
idea is that prophecy is an actual message or oracle
from God. The word is not used in the New
Testament to refer to the interpretation of an oracle
by a skilled interpreter. "In short, prophecy in Paul
cannot denote anything other than inspired speech.
And prophecy as charisma is neither skill nor
aptitude nor talent; the charisma is the actual
speaking forth of words given by the Spirit in a
particular situation and ceases when the words
cease."[15]

This distinction between prophesying and preaching is
consistent with Paul's discussion of prophetic utterance
in 1 Corinthians 11–14. When we examine the inspired
dimensions of the spiritual gifts of 1 Corinthians 12–14,
there is no reason to think the nature of prophecy in 1 Corinthians 11:4–5 is different. To use this passage to argue
that since women prophesied in Corinth, women are allowed to proclaim the gospel in public worship does not
follow. Preaching in the church is honored over prophecy
in Paul's writings because of its strategic place in God's
economy, and Paul reserves it for men.

Prophecy, writes Grosheide, "may offer divine instruction which is helpful . . . , but it is put beneath the apostolic preaching, beneath the gospel, which must occupy
the place of honor (compare I Cor. 12:28)."[16]

Now let's consider the second question: What distinctions were made between men and women in the activity
of prophesying? Apparently certain women were proph-

esying at Corinth in public worship[17] without covering their heads. The apostle considered such practice to show a lack of respect for their husbands[18] or for the men in the Corinthian congregation in general. The women's reasoning may have been a logical conclusion based on culture, since in Greek worship women were allowed to worship with loose hair, indicating they belonged to "the god" and not to the husband when they worshipped. Women in the church may have believed that certainly in Christ the order of creation and thus male authority within marriage were of no consequence.[19] The Corinthians desired to operate in the present as though the consummation of all things in Christ had already come, and the order of creation had been superseded.[20]

Therefore, in order to preserve the order he argued in 1 Corinthians 11:3, Paul taught that men should not wear a covering while praying or when moved upon by the Spirit to utter divine truth to the congregation. Women, on the other hand, could function in a prophetic role, but in order to preserve the social order given by the Creator, they must wear a sign of their subordination.[21] Nothing concerning church leadership or teaching men is found in the verse.

## Paul's Theological Reasons for His Teaching

The apostle said, in essence, that the woman is morally bound[22] to follow his instruction on covering her head when prophesying, whereas the man is morally bound to keep his head uncovered. This moral obligation has two primary bases and one secondary basis.

First, man is the image and glory of God, while woman is the glory of man. The word used here for *image* essentially means to be "similar" or "like."[23] To be in the image of someone is to be a representation of them. On the other hand, *glory* signifies "brightness," "splendor," or "honor."[24]

Based on this understanding, woman brings honor to the man by fulfilling her role of subordination and viceregency with him, while man brings glory to God by fulfilling the role of leader in God's creation. But why is man alone viewed as having the "image" of God in this passage? This can partly be explained by looking to the source of Paul's teaching here. One might think the image theme directly relates to Genesis 1:26–28. The apostle most likely derived his thinking, however, from the entire *dominion* (ruling) theme of Genesis 1.

One writer summarizes this concept well:

> Man, in his authority relation to creation and to woman, images the dominion of God over creation (a central theme of Gen. 1) and the headship of Christ over his church. The woman has a corresponding but different role to play. The woman is not called to image God in the relation which she sustains to her husband; she is rather to show loving obedience (Eph. 5:22). It would be inappropriate to identify her as the image of God in her relation to her husband, although . . . she does rule over creation with him.[25]

Woman is to be the glory of man. And just as the degree to which the man properly exercises the position God has assigned him determines his ability to bring glory to God, the degree to which the woman functions within the liberties and responsibilities assigned to her determines her ability to bring glory to man.

The woman's need to bring glory to man is attested in Proverbs 11:16, a passage similar in emphasis to Paul's instruction. Annié Jaubert goes further in her assessment by arguing that a man dishonored by a non-glorifying wife is hindered in his worship of God:

> If in the thought of Paul it is by Christ that the man renders glory to God (cf. II Cor 1:20) and that he must do honor to Christ, one could think similarly that it is by the man that the woman renders glory in the worship and she ought to do honor to him. The woman is referred to the man because, says Paul, it is not the man who comes from the woman, but the

woman who comes from the man; moreover the man was not created because of the woman, but the woman because of the man, an evident allusion to Gen. 2. One must without doubt deduce from this that for the man to be able to render to God a proper worship, for him to be the glory of God, it is necessary that he be without shame and therefore that the woman do him honor.[26]

Paul's reasoning was based on a theology of creation rather than on social and cultural considerations. His statement that woman is from the substance of man and man's need was the reason she was created (v. 8) clearly reflects the narrative of Genesis 2. Man's position of authority over woman is based on his priority in creation and thus on his being the image of God. The woman is the glory of her husband when she stands in proper relation to him within her created role.

Paul's emphasis in verses 2–9 was the issue of authority, which the Corinthians apparently had cast aside. Paul found it necessary to correct this error by demonstrating the need for these Christians to maintain the order of creation, even though men and women were equal in Christ (Gal. 3:26–28). As Jaubert comments, "Paul argues from an order of the creation, but of a creation reassumed by Christ."[27]

Lest the role of women in this new order be obscured, the apostle began a transition in verse 10: "For this reason the woman ought to have a *symbol* of authority on her head, because of the angels." Women, because of the angels, are to have authority on their heads. But exactly who are the angels, and what is the authority that women are to have on their heads? Biblical scholars offer several ideas concerning the identification of the angels in verse 10.[28]

Two major views include the idea that the angels are evil angels who would attack women whose heads are uncovered;[29] and the theory that the angels are good angels who observe the decorum and worship of the saints.[30]

Rather than getting bogged down in arguments that are really secondary to the solution of women's prophetic role at Corinth, our best solution is to look at the phrase *because of the angels* in light of the other occurrences of "angels" in 1 Corinthians. Paul used the term four times, more than in any other letter and "in each [passage] issues are raised which tie the angels in with the central problems of Corinth."[31]

Notice the prevalence of angels in 1 Corinthians. In contrast to the Corinthians' belief that they had "arrived" as Christians, Paul said all believers are in a cosmic "spectacle" (4:9) before angels. The present position of Christians is one of suffering, not one of exaltation and reigning. In chapter 6, verses 1–8 he chided them for going to court against other believers and reminded them that they were to judge angels, a fact of which they were aware.[32] First Corinthians 13:1 speaks of the languages of angels. The Corinthians felt they had become as the angels (Matt. 22:30), which may answer why some desired celibate lives.

And then in 1 Corinthians 11:10, the apostle desired to win women to obedience because of the high place woman occupies in relation even to the angels. In light of their high regard, he wanted them to know that when they uncovered their heads, seeking an authority not given to them in creation, it was a sign of rebellion and disgrace. On the other hand, covering their heads while prophesying served as a sign of their high position or authority above the angels.

What is the authority, then, that woman properly exercised with covered head?[33] The term the apostle used was *exousia*. Since Paul's argument up to verse 10 emphasized the subordination of women, many scholars have taken the term to be a sign of her husband's authority. However, as Hooker comments, this sense is strange, for then "the headcovering is not understood as a symbol of authority but, quite the reverse, as a symbol of subjection."[34] Jaubert considers this a major problem, asserting: ". . . the philological difficulty is enormous, since the expression

. . . in Greek never has the passive sense (undergo a domination) but always the active sense: possess a power."[35] Similarly, Ramsay called this view, ". . . a preposterous idea which a Greek scholar would laugh at anywhere except in the New Testament, where (as they seem to think) Greek words may mean anything that commentators choose."[36]

Most likely *exousia* stood for a sign of the woman's authority. She had a right to function prophetically in the new age when she had her head covered (either her hair put up or some other form of covering), and she operated as a vice-regent with man in the world and in the Church.

This understanding of *exousia* (1) retains the full force of the active sense of *exousia*; (2) fits the transitional movement of Paul at this juncture of his presentation in which he hopes to show the equality of man and woman in the midst of the discussion on subordination; (3) shows that Paul is arguing very carefully, in order to win over the women's obedience by showing them their high place in the old as well as the new creation.

So then, on the one hand Paul sought to build a foundation for the subordination of the woman to the man; and on the other hand he demonstrated the interdependence of the two. To do this he clearly signaled a limitation to the former argument.[37] Why did he change direction? Jewett would have us believe Paul realized the strong subordination he had been teaching was incompatible with the gospel expounded in Galatians 3:28: "Here we have what may be the first expression of an uneasy conscience on the part of a Christian theologian who argues for the subordination of the female to the male."[38] says Jewett.

A better answer is that the apostle desired to put in proper perspective the positional and functional relationships of man and woman before God. Ralph Alexander writes:

> Paul wants the men to understand clearly that though the woman is to be subordinate, she is not

inferior. They should not overpress the arguments of vv. 3–10 to the exclusion of woman's equality. Both man and woman are mutually interdependent upon one another for the continuing process of procreation. After the initial creation, man now comes through the woman, though the source of the woman was the man. Most important of all is that they not become proud of their roles, but remember that all things find their ultimate source in God. There is not place for 'lording it' over the woman in this context.[39]

So then, though in God's design woman was created for man, the woman and man are equal in essence and interdependent through God's design in procreation.

As we have seen, Paul based his view of the functional relationships between man and woman upon theological considerations from the creation narratives. This is also true in verses 13–15 regarding his argument from nature. He is appealing not to social custom[40] but to creation, a theme that has permeated the section. He clearly expects his original readers to understand and to concur with his judgment. Contending that this verse and those that follow are a retreat by the apostle because his position is weak[41] is indefensible. He has plainly established his thinking, and he assumes the evidence in the created order is clear enough for his readers to readily agree with him.

## The Practice of the Churches

Paul's conclusion in verse 16 was built on his pointed question in verse 13. In answer to that question, "Is it proper for a woman to pray to God with her head uncovered?" we must answer a resounding, "Certainly not!" if we are to make any sense of Paul's whole discussion. To those who still remained argumentative and unconvinced, the apostle appealed to the universal practice of the congregations of God (4:14–21). The church at Corinth was not to raise its head above the accepted tradition of all God's people elsewhere by rejecting the apostle's mandate. No other church had women who prophesied uncovered, and neither should their assembly.

Women experienced considerable freedom in the church of the first century, but that freedom was not permitted by the apostle Paul to contradict the order of creation, as was being done by many women in pagan religions.

Instead, the apostle sought to provide the opportunity for women to participate in the life of the church through prayer and prophecy. These were not expressions of authority in the same sense as the proclamation of revelation; prophecy seemed to consist of worship rather than teaching in the first century church. Even when women prophesied, however, they were to wear an indicator of authority and so not dishonor their husbands by acting independently of his authority.

Paul did not base his teaching on mere opinion or rabbinic bias. He clearly founded his teaching on the creation order, the function of the church in instructing angels of God's work in the church, and the uniform practice of the church throughout the Roman Empire—in whom also dwelt the Spirit, and obviously His leading.

## CAN WOMEN PRAY IN THE ASSEMBLY?

### The Principle of Prophecy and Prayer

As has already been shown, women were allowed to pray in 1 Corinthians 11, as a subcategory of prophesying, demonstrated by the juxtaposition of the two words *prophesy* and *pray* in that passage and the examples of Anna and Simeon in the Book of Luke.

Some scholars have sought to disallow women from praying in the congregation based on the teaching of Paul in 1 Timothy 2:8, to which we will now turn our attention.

### Men Praying in the Assembly

In Paul's exhortation to pray in verses 1–7, he instructed the men[42] of the congregation to pray in an exemplary manner. Then he turned his attention to the women at Ephesus with specific commands on teaching and authority. J. W. Roberts argues that women are excluded from the public prayer, writing:

> The *men* are to do the praying. Paul uses the specific word for the male—the man (husband) as opposed to the woman (wife). (The word is *aner* in Greek, not the generic word *anthropos*, which would have included both sexes.) This has the force of excluding the woman from leading the prayer in the assembly. That this is the correct understanding is plain from Paul's going on to apply the same limitation to the woman's teaching.[43]

Roberts' position on the use of *aner* appears substantial. However, Paul's use of the word would not preclude the option of women praying in the assembly any more than the use of the same word in 1 Corinthians 11:4 would preclude the woman of 1 Corinthians 11:5 from praying, except that the latter referred to inspired prayer and prophecy, and women were given explicit permission in that instance.

Dibelius and Conzelmann, contrary to Roberts, contend that the force of the argument lies in the word "likewise." The "likewise" would make the statement to the women in verse 9 parallel to the statement to the men in verse 8: "Likewise, also, I desire the women to pray." Thus women should be allowed to pray in the church.[44]

The option affirmed by Dibelius and Conzelmann is the very one rejected by Alexander, who says, "The infinitive which expresses Paul's desire for the woman is . . . 'to adorn.' There is no reason to assume the infinitive . . . 'to pray' in verse 9 (from v. 8) when an infinitive is given in verse 9."[45]

The second part of Roberts' argument, that the limitations set on a woman's teaching apply also to public prayer, may likewise be incorrect. The passage is similar to 1 Corinthians 14:36, where women are forbidden to ask questions. If a woman cannot speak publicly, the argument goes, then logically she cannot pray in public. This argument is not as convincing as the former, however. The apostle's reference to teaching is very explicit and is fostered by Scripture, while the question of women praying or not praying is somewhat vague, and has not been substantiated by Paul's presentation of theology.

## CONCLUSION

What can we conclude, then, from Paul's instruction concerning the place of women to pray in the assembly? Is it permissible, for example, for a woman to offer the morning prayer during a worship service? May a woman open a home Bible study or a Sunday school class with prayer? In each case the answer would have to be affirmative.

In fact, because of the distinctions Scripture clearly makes between a prophesying/praying role and a preaching/teaching role, it should be clear by now that women today are regularly excluded from many experiences in the church even though the Bible gives them great latitude to participate. Though the apostolic-age experience of direct revelation through prophecy is no longer in effect today, public prayer by a woman of the congregation should be no less enthusiastically received than public prayer by a man. Likewise, a word of testimony offered by a woman, or the reading of the Scriptures, or the reading of Scripture offered with a word concerning the Lord's work in her life should not be denied the godly, qualified woman.

The ministry of authoritatively expounding and proclaiming the written Word of God is the one that falls most definitively within the confines of biblical restriction for women. It is not a restriction based on superiority versus inferiority, nor of privileged status versus deprivation. It is a restriction based on divinely assigned role, for reasons that abide with the Creator Himself, left only to us to obey or ignore.

## CHAPTER EIGHT

# Should Women Teach Sunday School or Bible Studies?

Paul began 1 Corinthians 14:33b–35 by referring to the universal practice of the Christian church concerning the proper function of women in the local assembly.[1] The churches agreed on these points: women are to be silent at church meetings, are not to speak, and are to submit themselves.

Paul's reasoning was based on two things—the practice of the church and the Law—and demonstrated he was not expressing personal opinion, as in 1 Corinthians 7. Instead, he appealed to guides that should have convinced the Corinthians to follow his directions. The words "as in all the churches of the saints" have a close logical arrangement[2] with verse 36, "or did the word of God come originally from you? Or was it you only that it reached?"

The point here was that the Corinthians were not to be prideful in their interpretation and application of Christian truth, nor to suppose they could operate in conflict with the rest of the Christian world. Paul desired all Christians to conform to certain Christian practices (1 Cor. 11:16; 14:33b, 36; 1 Tim. 2:8). Therefore, to think the prohibitions Paul gave regarding women's participation in the church applied only to the Corinthians does not harmonize with Paul's appeal that *they* were to conform to the *rest* of the Christian church.

The idea today that current culture allows us to frivolously go against the last two thousand years of Christian teaching (heretical movements excepted) on the subject of women is very similar to the Corinthians' attitude. These injunctions from the apostle were not merely personal whim, nor were they based on custom. Instead, Paul said they were in agreement with the Scriptures.

## WHAT IS THE "LAW" IN PAUL'S DISCUSSION?

What exactly is the "law" to which Paul referred? Several writers (Barrett, Meyer, Orr, Godet)[3] consider it a reference to Genesis 3:16. F. F. Bruce believes the reference in 1 Corinthians 14:34 is to the creation narratives of Genesis 1 and 2.[4] The most comprehensive view is that Paul was using the entire teaching of the Torah as the basis of his position on female subordination, with the creation narratives providing the divinely ordained starting point.[5]

Regardless of the way we view the Old Testament foundation on which Paul built his argument, one point is clear: Paul was *not*, as some claim, unconsciously parroting Jewish tradition. He perceived his teaching as Christian teaching, backed by the Law. In verse 37 of 1 Corinthians 14 he said that all the things he had written were a command of the Lord. Whether we should see this as a reference to all of chapter 14 or only to verses 33b–37[6] is difficult to determine; either way, however, the command included his teaching on women.

Women[7] were commanded to be silent. This silence was not intended to inhibit their learning of Christian truth, since they could learn[8] from their husbands at home (v. 35). Rather they were not to be vocal in the assembly, which would be unsubmissive.

## ARGUMENTS ON THE SILENCE OF WOMEN

At this point various scholars have offered several explanations to alleviate an apparent discrepancy between 1 Corinthians 11:2–16 and 14:33b–35, and to define the nature of the speaking mentioned in the latter passage. Since the passage prohibits women from speaking in the church, on the surface it appears contrary to the teaching in 1 Corinthians 11:2–16, where women were allowed to pray and prophesy. Many critics eliminate the apparent contradiction by dismissing 14:33b–35 as an unauthoritative interpolation, a corruption of the text, added either by some anonymous author or by someone influenced by the 1 Timothy 2 passage.[9]

As discussed in Chapter 2, however, the verses are not inappropriate to the context or flow of the passage. They do not interrupt the movement of the passage, and in fact they speak further to the problem of proper order in the church meeting. The concern for this kind of order and unity is found throughout 1 Corinthians 14:26–40, and to attribute 14:33b–35 to a later editor or author, we would have to discount the entire section of 1 Corinthians. In reality, verses 35–36 fit quite well into the theme of the section. Moreover, the verses reflect the apostle's hand, not that of some later redactor or editor.

Another method of solving the supposed conflict is to view 14:33–34 in a church setting and 11:2–16 in a private setting (Grosheide, Gordon Clark, Alexander).[10] For example, one writer argues that the prophesying of women in 1 Corinthians 11 was *outside* the church meeting and 1 Corinthians 14 was *within* a church meeting. He says that although the praying and prophesying of 1 Corinthians 11 is undoubtedly public, there is no indication that they occur in the official services of the church, whereas the activity discussed in 1 Corinthians 14:33b–35 clearly does.[11]

But this view has substantial problems. Though verses 2–16 are an outgrowth of Paul's theme of abusing freedom in Christ, so are verses 17–34, as well as much of the rest of 1 Corinthians. Moreover, the use of "I praise you" in verse 2 and "I do not praise you" in verse 17 tie these two sections together structurally. They serve as a unit even as chapter 10 does.

The question of praying and prophesying is more naturally seen within a public worship setting in a letter largely addressed to Corinth's worship problems. The instruction is related directly to the need to conform to the practices of the other Christian congregations; thus it is certainly an issue of public worship.

## THE NATURE OF SPEAKING IN 14:33b–35

The meaning of the Greek word *laleo (speak)* has been a point of contention among scholars in the interpretation of 1 Corinthians 14:33b–35. Various scholars have interpreted the prohibited speaking as inspired speaking (prophecy or tongues); disruptive talk (gossiping or asking questions during worship); speaking out of turn (women attempting to take the male role in church); judging of the prophets; or all speaking in general.

### Inspired speaking

Some believe the public speaking prohibited to women in this passage is inspired speaking, that is, direct prophecy or the biblical gift of tongues. Joseph Dillow says that women are not permitted to exercise the gift of tongues in church and argues that a majority of tongues-speakers today are women, in direct violation of this passage.[12]

It is true that verses 34–36 follow a lengthy presentation on speaking in tongues, but it is incorrect to assume that *lalein* must be restricted to that phenomenon. The more immediate context is self-control and judging of prophets; but the prohibition on women speaking must be even broader since it stems from the teaching of the Law concerning women. Since Paul allowed inspired utterance if done under proper guidelines (1 Corinthians 11:2–16), surely he would allow it here as long as those guidelines were followed.[13] The Law required women not to occupy authority over men—something not involved in inspired utterance[14]—so the prohibition was apparently intended to curb a non-inspired usurping of authority rather than inspired speaking.

## Disruptive speaking

Another writer, Boyce Blackwelder, views the prohibited speaking in 1 Corinthians 14 as disruptive questioning of husbands by their wives. He offers several arguments for this. First, Paul used *laleo* rather than *lego*, the former meaning merely to utter sounds. Second, Paul used the present infinitive *lalein*, grammatically signifying continuous action. The women were not permitted to continue "la-la-ing" (Blackwelder's depiction of chatter). Third, the prohibition not to ask husbands questions in church logically carried with it the permission to ask at home. At last, a particular situation in the church might have existed that required the instruction—that is, women were disturbing the church service by trying to ask questions of their husbands.[15]

The perspective that *lalein* is chatter or asking questions has some historical credibility. Women and men were likely separated in worship in the church meetings in the same way they were separated in the synagogue.[16] But such a view does not account for the apostle's development of this passage from the Law, and thus is probably too narrow an interpretation. Neither does Paul's rule seem to be directed at particular disruptions in the Corinthian assembly. *Women are to be silent*, he says, *because they are women, not because they are disorderly.* His argument is that such speaking is contrary to the practice of the churches (14:33b) and is contrary to the Law of God which commands female subordination.[17]

In order to be subordinate, as the Law says, women are not to speak. If they violate this teaching of the Law, they annul the Law which commands subordination;[18] this is a reason for shame (v. 35).

Moreover, the mention of *lalein* as a reference to disruptive chatter does not agree with the use of the word in New Testament times. Though *lalein* was used of chatter in Classical times, in the New Testament period it was synonymous with *lego*.[19]

On the surface, we might think the meaning of *lalein* is determined by the instruction to ask husbands at home. But other factors need to be considered. Bruce says, "It is doubtful, however, whether such expressions as *they are not permitted to speak* and *it is shameful for a woman to speak in church* can be understood to mean no more than this."[20] Verse 35 is probably not included to define *lalein* exactly, but to counter a possible objection.[21] Godet has the right idea:

> The . . . [phrase] *and moreover if,* which begins ver. 35, introduces not a simple explanation, but a gradation: 'And even if they would learn something, they ought to abstain from asking in the congregation; they should reserve their questions to be submitted to their husbands in private.' The form . . . *and if,* is therefore founded on the fact that questioning was the case of least gravity, the one which seemed most naturally to admit of exception. But this very exception Paul rejects; for he knows how easily, under pretext of putting questions, women could elude the prohibition which forbade their public speaking.[22]

### Speaking out of turn

Some scholars contend that the injunction against women speaking in the church was aimed at a specific group of women within the church who were abusing their newfound freedom in Christ and seeking to exert authority over their husbands by contradicting them in the assembly.[23]

Though the suggestion that Paul was dealing with such a group of women at Corinth has some merit, it does not follow that his admonitions would be so limited. For example, he presented a need for the Corinthians to conform to the other churches in this practice (14:34b).[24] Moreover, the prohibition against women speaking in the church reveals an established practice.[25] And finally, his mention of the Law reveals the theological dimension of his command. In other words, his teaching was not designed merely to curb a current sociological crisis.

### Judging the Prophets

A variation of the "asking questions" position is posited by Seeberg, who takes *lalein* as "critical discussion of passages from the prophets. . . . Questions asked for the purpose of achieving deeper comprehension and of obtaining additional elucidation and confirmation of things heard."[26]

This approach is also taken by Hurley, who says that since Paul commanded the prophets to evaluate their messages to make sure no false doctrine was present, and since women were enlisted among the prophets, a problem of subordination to men had arisen.[27]

Because the context allows for the prohibited speaking to mean the evaluating of prophetic utterance, this view has much to commend it. Seemingly after the prophets spoke, other prophets would judge the utterance. If this position on the question is correct, then women were disallowed the opportunity to judge the prophets because such a practice would place them over the male prophets.

### Paul's Meaning in 1 Corinthians 14:33b-35

Though each of the foregoing interpretations have merit, all of them are too narrow for Paul's use of *lalein* in the context of 1 Corinthians 14:33b-35. These interpretations put the emphasis on the prohibition of disorder in the Corinthian assembly: loud talking, tongues-speaking, asking questions, or arguing with husbands. But both Grosheide[28] and Bruce[29] point out that *lalein* almost certainly means more than simply speaking during a service. It would seem more reasonable, then, that Paul's emphasis was on God's intention for women in general—namely, subordination to men in the sphere of spiritual authority. The term appears to be a broad, general prohibition that includes all of the alternatives offered above. And to prevent the Corinthians from moving to an extreme, such as forbidding women to study and learn period (or perhaps because they brought up the issue in their letter), Paul says women may learn from their husbands at home.[30]

This is not to imply that the prohibition applies only to married women. We should understand that unmarried women have both fathers and older women (Tit. 2:3–5) of whom they may ask questions.[31]

Paul's instruction was intended for all churches, and apparently was practiced by them. The Corinthians were commanded to get in line with the rest of the people of God. This apostolic instruction, which transcends culture, was based on the Old Testament's view of female subordination. Therefore, to act in disharmony with God's revelation was, and is, shameful.

Clearly the speaking referred to in 1 Corinthians 14 gave women an insubordinate role over men in the congregation. As Godet says, "The term *speaking in the church*, especially in a chapter where it is applied throughout to the glossolaletes and prophets, can only designate a public speaking, which has for its end to teach and edify."[32]

Some might argue that this reading contradicts 1 Corinthians 11, where Paul allowed women to pray and prophesy if their heads were covered. In that passage, however, women were in a state of inspiration, whereas in 1 Corinthians 14:33b–36 they were not. Those who spoke under inspiration were not expressing their own authority[33] and so were not in violation of the Law. Paul, in denying public address to women, also denies judging of prophets and public disagreement with husbands. Therefore any non inspired public speaking would be in violation of Paul's prohibition in 1 Corinthians 14:33b–36.

# THE PROHIBITION AGAINST WOMEN TEACHING

## Women Teachers in 1 Timothy 2:8–15

The teaching of Paul in 1 Timothy 2:8–15 appears to have more in common with 1 Corinthians 14:33b–35 than it has with 1 Corinthians 11:2–16 concerning the role of women in the church. While 1 Corinthians 11:2–16 recognized the prophetic function of women under the control of the Spirit, 1 Timothy 2:8–15, alongside 1 Corinthians 14:33b–35, prohibited a woman's vocal expression or position of leadership over men in the congregation.

These latter two passages are very similar in emphasis. The overriding thrust of the letter to Timothy was proper behavior in the church meeting (3:15),[34] especially regarding prayer and in 1 Timothy 2:8–15, speaking. The same is true of the Corinthian passage. And, as in 1 Corinthians 14:33b–35, the apostle's exhortation, though written to a specific location, was addressed to the Christian church in general.

## Feminist Arguments for Limited Application

Whether Paul's comments in 1 Timothy apply only to a local problem at Ephesus or to the total Christian church is, in fact, of considerable importance to our discussion on the role of women in the church. As noted in Chapter 2, some have argued that Paul was addressing a particular problem at Ephesus, where certain women were either teaching unorthodox views in the congregational meetings or at least were deceived by them. In view of this, the theory goes, Paul temporarily forbade women at Ephesus to participate vocally in the church meetings, either in teaching/preaching or in discussion.[35]

Evangelical feminists present several lines of argument to support this position (see Chapter 2 for a more detailed statement and refutation of these views). First, proponents argue that Paul's use of the term *permit* is to be understood as an opinion and as a temporary, localized injunction. Under different circumstances women would be allowed to teach in the congregational meetings; if Paul intended his instruction on this subject to be universal and permanent, he would have used different phraseology.

Second, proponents of this position claim that teaching was understood as open to all believers, not restricted to any particular church office. Priscilla is set forth as an example of a woman functioning as a teacher.[36]

Third, those who endorse this reading of the passage argue that the prohibition against women teaching is temporary, based on their interpretation of the term for *usurp authority*. Philip Payne argues that the term means "to dominate" or "to lord it over" men in the church, in contrast with the "quietness" advocated in 1 Timothy 2:11–12 and with "subjection" in 2:11. Women are not denied authority over men, he says; they are simply not to dominate men.[37] Hommes agrees with this view, saying that *usurp authority* means "to be bossy."[38]

Fourth, the same scholars suggest that Paul's use of *for* should not be taken as a casual conjunction, but rather as explanatory. Payne writes: "If [for] in 1 Tim 2:12 is explanatory, not illative, the actual *reason* Paul was prohibiting women in Ephesus from teaching is not that Eve was formed after Adam or that she was deceived by Satan, but that some women in Ephesus were (or were on the verge of becoming) *engaged in false teaching*."[39]

Fifth, some proponents of this view, including Spencer, claim that the presence of women at the Ephesian church who were either teaching error or captivated by it supports the conclusion that the instruction here was temporary and localized. Paul's purpose in 1 Timothy was to warn against unorthodox teachings toward which the Ephesian women were inclined.[40] This conclusion is further supported by Paul's use of the word for "gullible women" in 2 Timothy 3:6, weak women who listened to the wrong persons and were deceived. Some men were reacting to the false teaching of these women by not allowing women to teach at all.[41] In view of this situation, the theory goes, Paul slowed down the move to the full equality of men and women he would have otherwise supported.[42]

## Answers to the Feminists' Arguments

While any expositor may claim the 1 Timothy passage implies only a temporary injunction, does it really? Paul's use of similar grammatical structure in other places did not always include qualifying phrases when he gave something other than a personal opinion. Compare Romans 12:1, where he wrote, "I urge you, brothers, in view of God's mercy, to offer your bodies as living sacrifices . . ." (NIV). Paul did not necessarily use the first person in this verse to restrict action. He used it to express personal appeal or authority,[43] certainly appropriate (if not demanded) in this personal letter to Timothy.[44]

Payne's contention that teaching was open to all believers in general betrays a misunderstanding of the nature of teaching in the first century church. Teaching in the first century concerned more than mere conveyance of information. Early Christian teaching, built on the Jewish model, involved more than imparting information or alternate views. The teacher gave his personal direction and exercised authority over the learner. The teacher expected the student to accept his teaching. Also, the authority the teacher exercised over the learner came from a distinct relationship between the two. Teachers were either heads of communities or masters who took in disciples. Instruction was accompanied by correction of those who strayed from the accepted teaching (cf. 1 Tim. 4:11; 4:16–5:2; 2 Tim. 4:1–4; Tit. 2:15; 3:8–11).[45]

One scholar, Theodore Jungkuntz, correctly comments that teaching was not the conveyance of a skill, but an expression of authority: "It was a governing function which took place within a committed relationship of headship and submission and which was accompanied by the correction of individuals who were not following the accepted 'teaching'."[46]

It seems clear that the proclamation of doctrine in the Christian congregation and other educational settings was reserved for men, to whom God has given representative authority in spiritual matters dealing with leadership.

Paul stressed the importance of this prohibition on women teaching by placing it in the emphatic position in verse 12. Women simply are not allowed to teach men, because to do so would inherently give them authority over men in the congregation. Of course, there is no problem with females teaching females. In fact, Paul elsewhere encourages older women to teach younger women (Tit. 2:3).

The contention that *usurp authority* means "to dominate" is a stronger argument than the previous two. The word is unique in the New Testament—it appears only here. Bauer's lexicon (in translation) allows "domineer" as a possible meaning, but "have authority" is listed first. Even if one understands the word as "dominate,"[47] it does not necessarily carry a negative connotation. Knight, who has done a thorough study of all the occurrences of the word in existing literature, confirms the meaning of "have authority" as the natural meaning.[48]

Payne's claim for an explanatory rather than a causal application of *for* is difficult to understand. First, that usage is extremely rare,[49] so we would need to see good reason in the context to prefer it over the usual understanding. Second, the move from the command or prohibition to the reason for the command or prohibition is quite common in Paul's writing[50] and naturally occurs with *for*. Third, Payne admits Paul is giving a *reason* for his prohibition. The force of the explanatory *for* is to give a detailed explanation of a previous statement, which verses 13 and 14 do not do. It is more reasonable to understand *for* as introducing the reason Paul was prohibiting women to teach in the church.

False teaching did exist at Ephesus, as Spencer says, though it is extremely difficult to ferret out kind and number.[51] If false teaching was the emphasis of his instruction in 2:8–15, certainly he would also have prohibited men from such teaching. The emphasis, however, was not on women teaching *false doctrines*, but on women teaching *men*. Paul's reasoning against women teaching men, then, did not originate with a specific problem in the church, though this may have been *a* reason for his instruction; instead the prohibition was based on his understanding of Scripture.

### The Origin of Paul's Teaching

As explained more fully in Chapter 2, Paul derived his thinking from the creation-fall narratives of Genesis. Paul insisted that the prior creation of Adam and the deception of Eve in the fall excludes women as teachers over men. We have already investigated the narrative of Genesis 2 and Paul's understanding of it: Paul's first basis for denying woman authority over man was that Adam was created first (1 Tim. 2:13); the second basis of his teaching was that Eve was deceived, whereas Adam was not (Gen. 3:6). Paul's presentation is wholly transparent. Women are to subordinate themselves to men and are not to seek the place of men in the congregation.[52] And the way in which a woman is to learn (versus teach) is in "quietness." Alexander says,

> This term [quietness] is employed elsewhere in the New Testament to stress an external quiet demeanor, as in Acts 22:2 when the Sanhedrin becomes quiet to hear Paul's address or in II Thessalonians 5:12 where busybodies are exhorted to work in a quiet fashion and to eat their own bread. The implication of the word is that women should learn quietly, not talking, but listening.[53]

The idea of quietness is very similar to the teaching of Paul in 1 Corinthians 14:33b–35. Paul's support for his instruction resides in the teaching of the Law, probably referring to Genesis 2 or, some think, Genesis 3:16.[54] Likewise, the instruction in the passage at hand again shows the basis for Paul's reasoning as the fact that Adam was made first. As seen before in 1 Corinthians 11:9, man's priority in creation is the foundation of his authority. Furthermore, the woman was deceived (1 Tim. 2:14), unlike the man whose eyes were apparently wide open (though Phyllis Trible implies Adam may have been in a daze).[55]

To Paul this excluded a woman from teaching doctrine in the church, lest she fall and lead men astray, as her mother Eve had done.

## How It Works in the Church

If we accept the Pauline position as fully inspired and consistent with the inerrant nature of Scripture, as well we should, we are left in a position of reconciling the existence of obviously gifted women in the body of Christ with the prohibition against their authoritative teaching of men. How do we account for the gifts and desires of godly women who sense their call to teach and who, by virtue of education, commitment, and effectiveness, indeed should be involved in some kind of teaching ministry?

First, that a woman possesses the gift of teaching does not automatically assume she will be or should be teaching men. If the Bible is consistent within itself, it will not be self-contradictory. That is to say, the bestowal of spiritual gifts on the one hand will not violate and contradict inscripturated apostolic teaching on the other. Likewise, Paul's instruction concerning women teaching men obviously would not run counter to his experience with Aquila and Priscilla, or to their ministry in Apollos' life, as recorded in Acts 18.

We must consider, then, what type of ministry women who are gifted in the area of teaching may have in the church today. May they teach in any context, so long as it is not a pulpit ministry on Sunday morning? May they teach a mixed Bible study, or assume a faculty post in a Christian institution of higher education?

Based on our study up to this point, we understand that Paul's prohibition on women teaching is specifically directed toward the authoritative exercise of spiritual authority, such as that of an elder, of women over men. Using the Word of God to reprove, rebuke, exhort, and call men to accountability before God is, according to Scripture, a male prerogative. And though the feminist position seeks to characterize this instruction as restrictive, demeaning, and narrow, teaching authority over men is but one facet of a much broader potential for women in ministry. It behooves the woman of God to consider the wealth of ministry opportunities available to her.

For example, though Scripture apparently does not allow a woman to authoritatively teach the Scriptures in a setting that would include a mixed or male audience, this does not mean a woman should not be able to give her testimony before the same group. It does not mean she cannot team with her husband in a ministry of discipleship and encouragement (as apparently Priscilla did with Aquila in Acts 18). It would further allow, of course, for a woman to teach authoritatively any size gathering of women, whether a home Bible study or an extremely large gathering such as today's Bible Study Fellowship groups.

A woman would also be aptly qualified to take an active part in any Christian education matters that would exclude the teaching of men. While teaching a mixed Bible study apparently would not be advisable for the woman who desires to conform to the biblical mandate, administrating a church's Christian education program probably would be (providing that position is not simultaneously an appointment to the board of elders, as it is in some churches). Teaching any group of non-adults obviously is an area where her gifts could be superbly employed; our culture's lamentable disbelief in the value of children does not make children's work a "second-class" ministry. Another area of service in dire need of talented, teaching-oriented women (and men) of God is the development of teaching materials and curricula.

As mentioned earlier, counseling is a ministry wide open to women who are willing to pursue the training necessary to be effective. While it might not be advisable for a woman to counsel a man, there is a great need for trained women who can counsel other women. Not only are men less equipped than women both to empathize and advise, an ever-present danger of romantic attachment by one or both parties exists when men counsel women. Counseling of couples by couples is a virtually untouched area of counseling, one that would be a viable and productive outlet for the woman whose gifts include an expertise in handling God's Word.

## CONCLUSION

In short, though feminists paint a caricature of Paul's prohibition on women teaching as demeaning, narrow, limiting, and restrictive, it can be as liberating and instructive as any other admonition of God's Word. Only within the boundaries of the Scriptures do we experience true freedom as believers, whether we are dealing with the sanctity of marriage, the qualifications of an elder, or the beneficiaries of a woman's gift of teaching.

## CHAPTER NINE

# Where May Women Minister in the Church Today?

May a woman pastor a church or serve on the board of elders or have some other equivalent ministry in the local church? May a woman be a deacon? May she be on a pastoral staff? These are but a few of the questions we need to address concerning Christian women in the churches today. Since women are equally made in the image of God and are equally gifted by the Spirit and called to the service of the Lord, we must be careful not to exclude them from any area of responsibility or service to which God has called them. In order to find what offices and ministries are biblically open to women, we will first look at the functions of elders, pastors, and deacons in the New Testament.

## THE FUNCTION OF AN ELDER OR PASTOR

First Corinthians 11:2–16 and 14:33b–35, as well as 1 Timothy 2:12, do not directly address the issue of women serving as the general pastor or elder (the overseer) of a local body of believers. But these passages do throw enough light on other scriptures—1 Timothy 2–5, 2 Timothy 4, and Titus 1—that we can draw some firm conclusions.

As we have discovered, women are fellow-laborers with men in the vineyard of God and in the world in general. They are equal image-bearers. It appears from a study of the pastoral epistles, however, that they are restricted from the office of elder or pastor. Let us examine why this is so.

Churches in the New Testament period were viewed as a group of Christian families come together for corporate worship and teaching. It was only natural that from among the husbands of the families came the leadership. Note that among the qualifications for an overseer (or pastor) was the requirement for the person to be the husband of one wife. Never is there the understanding of an overseer being the wife of one husband. A man is assumed for the office. Moreover to be a leader in the church the overseer or elder must rule over his own home in a proper manner. If he could not do this, then how could he rule in the church of God? It is clear that capacity for rule in the church depended upon the capacity and performance of a similar kind of rule at home. A woman could not fulfill this strategic qualification for church office since she was not allowed such rule over the home.

A second duty of an overseer was to instruct the local church in the Word. The elders were the ones who oversaw doctrine in the local community of believers. Based upon the authority of the Word of God, they were to reprove, rebuke, correct, and instruct in righteousness. Women were not given such a charge. In fact, according to 1 Corinthians 14:33b–35 and 1 Timothy 2:12, they were prohibited from such activity. Timothy, as the teaching elder, or pastor if you prefer, was given the responsibility of this type of instruction (2 Tim. 4:2).

As mentioned briefly in Chapter 8, the idea of teaching in New Testament times meant something more than it does today. Clark (pp. 196–197) observes:

Modern "teaching" does not involve the exercise of authority over people, except insofar as the teacher needs to maintain enough discipline to continue teaching. Modern "teaching" is usually a process whereby an expert is hired to transmit a skill or information to students who are free to ignore what is taught.

By contrast, the early Christian understanding of teaching, built upon the Jewish understanding, saw teaching as an activity involving personal direction and an exercise of authority. The teacher did not just give his views. He laid out what he expected the student to accept.

Moreover, teaching occurred within a relationship in which the teacher had authority over the student. The focus of teaching in the New Testament was upon teaching a way of life. Students were expected to follow that way of life, and the teaching was passed on with authority. Teachers were either elders, heads of a community or of some grouping within the community, or masters who took in disciples who submitted themselves for formation. Teaching was not a function in which an expert came and performed a service which a client was free to receive or not receive as he wished. The teaching occurred within a relationship in which the students acknowledged the teacher's authority. Moreover, authority was primarily exercised within the early church not as much by individual direction, but by teaching given to a body, accompanied by the correction of individuals who were not following the accepted teaching (cf. 1 Tim. 4:11, 4:16–5:2; 2 Tim. 4:1–4; Titus 2:15, 3:8–11). In other words, the Scripture views teaching primarily as a governing function, a function performed by elders, masters, and others with positions of government. In this context, the connection between teaching, exercising authority, and being subordinate can be seen more clearly.

Clark thus clarifies the meaning of "teaching" in the first century church and in the world at large during this period of history. Teachers expected their students to learn and obey their teaching. Paul develops the same idea of teaching in the letters of 1 and 2 Timothy and Titus. In Titus 1 elders are told to rebuke and to stop the mouths of those who subvert sound teaching. Certainly women may have this ministry over other women, but not over men, for they would be functioning as an elder to do so.

## Is there an office of deaconess?

Women may very possibly have exercised positions of responsibility in the local churches of the first century. Romans 16:1 calls Phoebe a servant of the church at Cenchrea. It is entirely reasonable to understand the word *servant (diakonos)* to mean the church office of deacon, and to conceive of Phoebe holding this position in the local church. Many scholars believe that the office of deaconess, rather than the role of the wives of deacons, is discussed in 1 Timothy 3:11, a position to which the author subscribes. The subsequent development of this role for women, as well as that of widow and virgin, is well attested in the second and third centuries as discussed in Chapter 5.

The office or ministry of deaconess was clearly existent in the post-apostolic age, but is poorly established in the New Testament.[1] Only two passages might suggest the office of deaconess, and both are obscure. The word *diakonos* occurs only in reference to Phoebe. It is certainly intended as a title of respect and commendation, and may have been used "because she distributed relief to the sick and the poor as he [Paul] and Barnabas had done when they as deacons, distributed the relief money to the famine sufferers in Jerusalem (Acts 11.29, 12.23).⁴ Should one, however, understand something more from the passage? Scanzoni and Hardesty argue that one should take the word *diakonos* and the word *prostatis* to indicate Phoebe held the office of deacon. Though Phoebe's title *diakonos* might simply indicate a servant, the term *pros-*

*tatis*, they conclude, refers to one who presides or rules over another.[3]

They are inaccurate on two counts. First, their conclusion is a misunderstanding of the office of deacon in the New Testament. Even if Phoebe was a deacon, in the New Testament the office was not a position of rule as was that of the elder. Note the words of Murray:

> Though the word for "servant" is the same as is used for deacon . . . it is also used to denote the person performing any type of ministry. If Phoebe ministered to the saints, as is evident from verse 2, then she would be a servant of the church and there is neither need nor warrant to suppose that she occupied or exercised what amounted to an ecclesiastical office comparable to that of the diaconate. The services performed were similar to those devolving upon deacons. Their ministry is one of mercy to the poor, the sick, and the desolate. This is an area in which women likewise exercise their functions and graces. But there is no warrant to posit an *office* than the case of widows, who prior to their becoming the care of the church, must have borne the features mentioned in 1 Timothy 5:9, 10.[4]

Second, the feminine word *prostatis*, related to the masculine *prostates*, a guardian or defender, is not used of Phoebe to mean one who rules. In Jewish literature the masculine word took on the meaning of the feminine, which meant patroness or helper.[5] Moulton and Milligan find no instance of *prostatis* in the papyri but list *prostates* as meaning leader, or chief man.[6] The idea of leader or patroness for the *prostatis* in Romans 16:1, however, is foreign to the context. The meaning of one who presides or is leader simply will not fit. Murray clarifies this:

> It is true that the masculine *prostates* can mean "ruler," "leader", "president" and corresponding verbs

*prostateuo* and *prostateo* have similar meaning. But
*prostates* can also mean 'patron' or 'helper'. The
feminine *prostatis* can have the same meaning.
Besides, the meaning 'president' does not suit in the
clause in question. Paul says that Phoebe 'became a
*prostatis* of many and of me myself.' Are we to
suppose that she exercised rule over the apostle?
What she was to the others she was to the apostle.
The rendering that Prohl adopts 'She was made a
superintendent of many by me myself' is wholly
unwarranted. Furthermore, the believers at Rome are
enjoined to 'stand by' or 'help' Phoebe (parastéte auté)
and the last clause in verse 2 is given as a reason to
enforce this exhortation. 'She herself was a helper of
many and of me myself.' There is exact
correspondence between the service to Phoebe
enjoined upon the church and the service she herself
bestowed upon others. The thought of presidency is
alien to this parallel.[7]

The passage in 1 Timothy 3:11 is even more problematic. The Staggs think the reference here is to wives of
deacons, because women are not permitted by Paul to
teach or have authority over men.[8] Colin Brown argues,
on the other hand, that the passage more likely refers to
deaconesses, since *gunaikas* occurs in the discussion of
the qualities desired for a deacon, the word *diakonos* oc-
curing before and after verse 11.[9] Since the deaconesses
do not necessarily have to exercise authority over men in
the congregation, the Staggs' argument loses much of its
force. Other scholars simply acknowledge the question
cannot be settled with certainty.[10]
Though the passage is not perfectly clear, Henry Alford
gives several good reasons for rejecting the view that it
refers to wives of deacons and favoring a reading that es-
tablishes an office of deaconess. Since there is no direct
reference to the deacons in the verse, one should not understand wives but deaconessess. The use of the expres-

sion *hosautos,* the same word by which the deacons were introduced before the mention of these women, indicates a new ecclesiastical class. In verse 11 the wives of the deacons are mentioned as a new subject, which would hardly happen if their wives were mentioned before. Although this writer disagrees, Alford also believes that the mention of Phoebe as a deaconess in Romans 16:1 adds weight to his argument.[11]

The office of deaconess is not certain in the New Testament church, but the preponderance of evidence is that women formally carried out this ministry, as is especially seen in the post-apostolic period.

This brings up a possible corollary question: May a woman be a paid member of a pastoral staff? To answer this, we need to recognize that the modern arrangement of a paid pastoral staff is an outgrowth of our culture, not a prescription of God's Word. The Bible prescribes the qualifications of overseers and deacons and advises men as well as women how to promote edification of the body. It also tells us that the worker is worthy of his wages. It does not, however, outline the procedure for setting up a church front office, complete with paid positions and an organizational chart.

What this means for us is *not* that such a structure is unbiblical, but rather that as long as we conform to what Scripture reveals, we may operate within *any* reasonable structure. In other words, a woman member of a church's pastoral staff is not a violation of Scripture. She may be a Christian education director, a visitation coordinator, chair of the missions committee, women's counselor—any of a number of positions in which she can function biblically and effectively without exercising spiritual authority over men as an elder would.

In fact, the opportunities biblically open to women far outnumber those that are limited to male leadership, and those godly and qualified women who serve in such ministries should be financially compensated just as liberally as are men.

## PRINCIPLES TO USE IN ESTABLISHING
## WOMEN IN MINISTRY

As we observed in the conclusion of Chapter 7, a biblical injunction against the exercising of spiritual authority by women over men can either be viewed from a negative perspective, as is the wont of feminists, or from a positive perspective.

Interestingly, though feminists charge biblicists with attaching values of superiority/inferiority to the exercising of teaching authority, it is they in fact who do so. Their desire for women to have the same responsibility for teaching men as men themselves do is based on a supposed position of superiority for the teacher. According to the Bible, the one thing primarily greater for the teacher is accountability before God: "My brethren," wrote James, "let not many of you become teachers, knowing that we shall receive a stricter judgment" (James 3:1). This is, of course, a universal accountability, not one reserved only for men who teach. Women who teach, whether in conformation to the Scriptures or otherwise, are under the same divine scrutiny and ultimate accountability as are men.

The exercise of authoritative teaching over men is but one facet of the overall scope of Christian service. Since the Scriptures confine that ministry to men only, the woman of God may either limit her ministry by her hardened resentment toward the one prohibition (ungodly behavior indeed), or expand her horizons to take in the full spectrum of ministry opportunities which are available to her.

For the woman willing to serve Christ by serving His people, and for the leadership of Christian ministries who long to see godly women used in His service, a number of principles should prevail in any decision concerning the placement of a woman in a ministry situation. These guidelines are not new, nor are they limited only to women. New Testament principles concerning the suitability of the servant for service (and for leadership) are universal. Those offered below are neither exhaustive nor restricted only to women, but they are important.

## Spiritual Qualifications

Perhaps it goes without saying, but placing a woman into ministry in order to "make a statement" about one's church, to meet some type of master plan or quota, or to equalize some supposed "power structure" in the church is a terrible mistake— as it is any time a male is given a position of leadership for any reason short of the spiritual qualifications outlined in Scripture. What standard do we use to determine spiritual qualifications, for men and women both? A good place to start is 1 Timothy 3:1–13 since the criteria listed there are predicated on a search for spiritual maturity in leadership. Another appropriate passage is 2 Timothy 2:21–26, which outlines characteristics of relational aptitude and the kind of even-temperedness required of anyone who deals with other believers on a daily basis.

## Pure Motives

If a man were to accuse a Christian woman, particularly a feminist, of "smiling her way" into organizational leadership in order to aid her ultimate feminist goals, the accusations of sexism and paranoia would be deafening. Yet feminist author Patricia Gundry, in her book *Neither Slave Nor Free* (p. 120), observes within a context of obvious sanction:

> One woman told me, "I smiled my way onto
> several committees in my church so I could be part of
> the decision-making body." She said she knew that in
> order to be effective [i.e. for feminism] as a lone
> individual she had to *do* something rather than wait
> for it to happen. She is an attractive and outgoing
> person. She used her personality to gain access to the

opportunity to help make decisions. Now she helps other women onto those committees. She also influences many small decisions in the direction that will aid her ultimate goal.

Fifth columns are generally reserved for warfare, and while feminists have openly declared war on any Christian institution that holds to what we have determined as a biblical view of women in ministry, the prudent body of believers will guard against the kind of double standard that condemns improper behavior on one hand yet promotes outright deceit on the other. Any hidden agenda—whether it be feminism, moral laxity, legalism, social activism, doctrinal adjustment, or liberalism—can quickly erode and destroy an entire leadership team. The Bible is clear that any leader, male or female, must have pure and transparent motives.

## A Proven Track Record

Of course, not every woman who desires to serve in some type of ministry position will have experience to go along with her desire. Yet time by itself can add a great deal of credibility to a person's potential by confirming spiritual commitment and proving true humility. Remember, 1 Timothy 3 stipulates that a leader should not be a "novice, lest being puffed up with pride he fall into the same condemnation as the devil."

Time also allows a believer's basic beliefs and doctrine to solidify and become evident in profession as well as practice. Aberrant theology, while it may make for lively discussions and interesting articles, has no place at the spiritual core of a church's ministry, whether to three-year-olds or thirty-year-olds.

A proven track record also includes the Christian's reputation in the "real world." This may not be much comfort to the recent Bible college graduate who wants to jump immediately into ministry, but it will safeguard that person's ministry and the reputation of Christ in his church.

## A Willingness to Serve

It is unfortunate that the Christian church has bought the bill of goods pandered by our culture—one that equates leadership with prestige, power, and respect. This was not Christ's view of spiritual leadership. His approach to service for the kingdom was one of other-centeredness rather than self-centeredness; of availability rather than unapproachability; of respect for others rather than a demand of respect from others; of being prepared to lead but willing to serve, rather than aspiring to leadership because of its supposed "high" position.

## Right Priorities

This may well be the "acid test" of one's suitability for ministry in any context. What is important to the person who aspires to leadership? Is it the opportunity to obey God's Word while taking the good news of salvation in Christ to every man, woman, and child possible? Is it the privilege of helping fulfill the Great Commission, whether by administrating the Christian education program of a church, teaching a Bible study for 200 women, or discipling three hungry young believers?

Preoccupations reveal priorities, whether or not we want our priorities revealed. For the woman who aspires to spiritual leadership and is preoccupied first with obedience to the Scriptures and second with fulfillment of Christ's Great Commission—little can stand in her way.

## THE MANY OPPORTUNITIES FOR WOMEN

Throughout Scripture, one message comes through loud and clear when we observe those whom God would use in His work. Male or female, He is interested in using those who are entirely submitted to His will as expressed in His Word. Opportunities abound for women who desire to serve the church. Our focus needs to center on the many ministries that are biblically open to all Christians and not on the few restrictions mandated by Scripture.

During Israel's wilderness wanderings, Korah and a following in excess of 250 rebelled against Moses and Aaron because they felt it was unfair these two should be designated leaders while others weren't. According to Numbers 16, in fact, they accused Moses and Aaron of considering themselves a cut above everyone else because of what God had commanded and permitted them to do. "For all the congregation are holy," they argued, "every one of them, and the Lord is in their midst; so why do you exalt yourselves above the assembly of the Lord?" (16:3).

Korah and his companions felt that because all believers are equal, their roles should be completely interchangeable, whether or not God had commanded otherwise. Equality, to Korah and his companions, meant complete interchangeability of roles. What they failed to realize, however, is that for reasons of His own, God had limited the role of the priesthood. Though everyone in the redeemed community—all those who had been redeemed from bondage in Egypt—were equal, God had chosen to assign different roles to different segments of that community.

Of course, God's directives did not prevent Korah from rebelling against that principle and bringing on himself and his followers the wrath of God. For our purposes, the punishment in this episode is not the point. The point is that God chose to assign distinctly different roles to co-equal members of the redeemed community. And He expected those roles to be honored.

In 1 Samuel 13:8–14, we find another episode in which someone assigned one role aspired to fill another role assigned to someone else. In this case, Saul had been chosen by God to be king over Israel. It was as high an office as existed in human terms, and in this case there could be no feelings of insecurity—or so one would think.

After a great military victory, however, Saul decided that his time and prestige were more important than the command of God. After waiting seven days for Samuel to show up and make offerings to the Lord, Saul presumed God did not really care about the distinction of roles and took it upon himself to assume the role of priest. After all, the people were scattering and needed to be reinforced spiritually. The offerings were ready. The people were waiting. And Saul *was* king, after all. Why shouldn't he take on just one more duty and perform the priestly function?

Why? Because God had assigned specific roles to specific people and groups of people, and He expected His commands to be honored. Once Saul had made his presumptuous move, Samuel showed up and said to him, "You have acted foolishly; you have not kept the commandment of the Lord your God, which He commanded you, for now the Lord would have established your kingdom over Israel forever. But now your kingdom shall not endure."

There are other examples in Scripture that indicate equality as persons, which the Bible freely attributes to all in the community of faith, does not necessarily presume interchangeability of roles. Within the context of human history, God chose to work His kingdom program through one man, Abraham, and his offspring. Yet that does not exclude anyone—Jew or non-Jew—from participating in His kingdom by faith. Within the nation of Israel, God limited the priesthood to the tribe of Levi, but that did not make any tribe superior or inferior to any other. And even among the Levites, anyone with a physical handicap was excluded from the priesthood—which in no way meant he was inferior to the able-bodied, nor that God considered him less than his brethren.

The Scriptures are clear that submission to the Lord is going to include some kind of submission on the human plane. The great error of many feminists is their assumption that submission equals inferiority and precludes equality—and that is just not true.

Consider, for example, Abraham's submission to Melchizedek. David submitted to Saul before ascending to Israel's throne, and to the voice of God's prophet afterward. Josiah submitted to the Law. Daniel submitted to a pagan government, except when it would clearly violate the Word of God. Jesus submitted to His parents, to the Law (though not the Pharisees' religiosity), and to the human government. Obviously, in not one of these instances did submission or difference in role assume inequality as persons.

In the New Testament, slaves are commanded to be submissive to their masters, though we well know that in Christ there is "neither slave nor free." Men are to submit themselves to the command to love their wives as selflessly and sacrificially as Christ loved the church. Wives are to submit to their husbands. And Christians are to submit to the government—an order penned during the abominable reign of Nero.

Again, none of these examples indicates that equality and difference of roles are mutually exclusive. The fact that we all are equal in Christ does not exempt us from being obedient to God's Word. Nor does His Word limit us in any way from experiencing complete fulfillment in our relationship with Him. Why not? Because our greatest fulfillment comes not in transgressing every limit and every boundary He has established, but in living in submission to Him, expressed in submission to the limit He has established. This is equally true for male and female, Jew and Greek, slave and free.

And how does all this help us better understand the myriad ministry opportunities open to godly, qualified women? More than anything else, it sets us free to look at every opportunity for service first in light of obedience to God's Word, then in light of the unlimited potential of every ministry pursued in a spirit of obedience and submission to Him.

What, then, of the godly woman who aspires to teach? Does the biblical injunction against the exercise of authoritative teaching over men mean she is forever doomed to an unfulfilled Christian life and relegated to second-class citizenship in the kingdom? Of course not!

The gifted female teacher can—and should—take every

opportunity to teach women, whether in small groups or large. She can train other women to do the same. I believe she has been divinely equipped to teach children far better than most men can. She can write. She can author Bible study materials. She can do personal evangelism and discipleship among women, as men should do among other men.

Does the biblical model preclude a woman from giving her testimony in a church meeting, or offering the Scripture reading, or making announcements, or leading songs, or offering a public prayer? These questions can be answered with another question: Are any of these ministries an expression of authoritative, elder-like teaching over men? It is obvious they are not, and thus they should not be excluded from the ministry opportunities afforded qualified women of God.

Can a woman fill an administrative role in which she has a vested supervisory authority over men? Again, recognizing the difference between the administrative authority of a supervisor or employer and the spiritual authority of an elder or teacher, it is apparent that a wide variety of administrative functions of ministry, within and outside, are biblically available to women.

Should a woman be placed in a teaching position in a Bible college or seminary where she would be teaching the Scriptures and theology to men? I would sensitively and understandingly say "no," based not on a professional or so-called "sexist" elitism, but solely on the admonitions of God's Word. Should she then hold only menial, insignificant, non-teaching positions? Absolutely not—not so long as there are godly women for her to teach, programs for her to administrate, Bible studies for her to lead, women for her to counsel; in other words, not so long as the institution continues to function as a multidimensional ministry.

The Holy Spirit has bestowed spiritual gifts on all members of the body of Christ. 1 Corinthians 12:4–11 indicates that various gifts have been distributed to believers; there is no reason to believe any gift is limited to men. In view of this, local churches must provide ways in which women along with men can exercise their spiritual gifts. Women must not be restricted to ministry with children, though certainly such a ministry is an honorable and necessary one for which God has especially enabled women through their maternal instincts. Women may be leaders in visitation to the sick, counseling other women and men, and leading Christian education programs, missionary programs, and evangelistic efforts.

Older women have special responsibilities toward younger women. They have a duty to teach the young women in Christian communities to love their husbands and their children, to act properly in their dress and demeanor, to be submissive to their husbands, and to fulfill their duties at home (Titus 2:4–5). The revered woman of Proverbs 31 acted in similar godly fashion, although, we are wise to remember, she was not restricted to these activities.

It is indeed unfortunate that an over-emphasis on trained male leadership fulfilling every aspect of ministry in the local church has excluded such "women elders of women" from serving Christ in a unique and valuable way by providing exemplary leadership for younger women. We needn't go into detail here about the risks and inadequacies inherent in the presumption that any and every male pastor is better equipped to counsel women in his church than are mature, godly Christian women in the same congregation. Suffice it to say that the pastoral staff that fails to draw on the biblical resource of qualified older women in the congregation to fulfill the church's ministry to younger women is not only risking the effectiveness of its ministry, it is operating in clear contradiction to the instruction of Titus 2:4–5.

This type of ministry needn't be a formalized extension of the duties of a pastoral staff. In a large city in central California, for example, a woman (appropriately named Faith) for years conducted an annual "feminar" for the area's Christian college women. The all-day seminar was actually an outgrowth of a para-church ministry led by Faith and her husband that was usually attended by a mixture of Christian young women from the community. Included in this godly, mature woman's teaching was a combination of material concerning Christian maturity as well as biblical womanhood. It was a successful ministry that simply could not have been effected by a man.

One church in the southwestern U.S. in recent years has made a transition from male pastoral staff counseling of women to counseling of women by a trained female staff. Since making the change, the success of the church's pastoral counseling has risen dramatically, a change everyone involved attributes to this small but biblical adjustment.

In one para-church organization, leadership by male directors over a mixed staff has been modified whenever possible so that both a director and his wife are responsible for the staff, he for the male staff and she for the female. Not only has this helped avoid romantic attachments and sexual pressures on all sides, but the effectiveness of training and accountability has also increased.

These are just a few examples, but the point is clear. With so many opportunities available for fulfilling clear biblical injunctions concerning female leadership, we should have precious little time left to force the application of questionable interpretations of Scripture into an already stressed context.

## CONCLUSION

In short, the question of where women may minister in the church of Jesus Christ is not a question of who is superior and who is inferior, who gets the "good work" and who gets the "leftovers," or who is "sexist" and who is "open-minded."

It is, in its very essence, for both men and women, a question of submission to the Word of God. The would-be leader who is not submissive to the Bible's adamant warnings against self-glorification and pride is not worthy to be a leader. The would-be leader who is not submissive to the Bible's clear teaching against greed is not worthy to be a leader. The aspiring teacher who is not submissive to the Bible's self-validation as inspired and inerrant, and who does not "rightly divide the Word of truth," is not to be a teacher.

And, no matter what it means in comparison to a contemporary social agenda—whether it be feminism, materialism, pacifism, socialism, imperialism, capitalism, racism, or any other "ism"—the would-be leader who is not entirely submissive to the liberating constraints of God's perfect Word should never be a leader at all.

# What Next?

Where has our study taken us? We have seen, both directly and indirectly, that today's feminist movement within evangelical circles is the outgrowth of a social agenda set by militant feminists in general. The feminist philosophy presumes that equality assumes interchangeability of roles, and is ultimately grounded in the belief that biblical interpretation should be determined by social norms and contemporary issues. Scripture, of course, supports neither of these notions.

We have seen that charges of "sexism" and "inequality" are freely hurled at individuals, churches, and organizations that resolutely hold to what they believe is the clear teaching of Scripture. As in the McCarthyism of post-World War II America, an accusation is as good as a conviction, and anyone who dares to disagree is fair game for attack. This is an unfortunate situation in the church of Jesus Christ, where the love of Christ should prevail.

Concerning treatment of the biblical text, the feminists have adopted a method of interpretation in which the meanings of words are "adjusted" according to obscure, sometimes even fabricated usages well outside the mainstream of a New Testatment context. Moreover, they make unfounded presumptions about the cultural setting of certain texts in order to interpret them in a manner more consistent with the feminist disposition. In some cases, Paul's spiritual maturity, and thus the inspiration and inerrancy of his inscripturated writings, is called into question, and in even more extreme cases we are asked to believe that Jesus was too limited by the culture and His

159

own upbringing to take the step of appointing a woman apostle.

Though this type of treatment foisted on the inspired text should speak for itself, we have taken the time to interact with the arguments of the evangelical feminists. Though the material offered here must by virtue of space and documentation limits be abbreviated, the author has sought to refer the reader to primary sources whenever possible. And he has attempted to demonstrate that a "normal," or historical/grammatical, interpretation of the Scriptures requires that one determine the meaning of key texts without dragging the excess baggage of social pressure or tradition in tow.

We have examined the historical situation of women in the time of the New Testament as well as looked into the ministry of women both in the New Testament and in the first three centuries of the church.

Most important, we have established the very biblical reality that men and women are indeed equal in created essence and are co-heirs and co-equal in Christ. We have further established the biblical corollary that equality rarely, if ever, assumes absolute interchangeability of roles, whether we are talking about men among men, family members within the family, subjects within a government, partners within a marriage, individuals within church government, or women and men in relation to leadership. This is indeed a difficult issue for feminists, since one of the basic tenets of feminism is that equality mandates an indistinguishability of roles, manners, characteristics, even, in the case of secular, militant feminism, sexual preference.

Those who believe in an unbiblical male dominance of all facets of ministry may be as dissatisfied with the author's conclusions as will be many feminists. But it is clear that the biblical limitations on women in ministry deal primarily with spiritually authoritative teaching by women over men, which leaves open far more possibilities than it excludes. We have seen that ultimate spiritual fulfillment for women, as well as men, is found not in achieving the highest possible position in a hierarchy, nor by gaining the greatest amount of latitude to function in any and every role, whether biblically prescribed or otherwise, but in submission to the will of God as revealed in His perfect Word.

It is abundantly clear for any who are willing to set aside their predetermined biases that the current wave of evangelical feminism assaulting the harmony and effectiveness of Christ's church is an outgrowth of the secular feminist movement. And while some elements of this movement provide positive aspects to recommend it (i.e. equity in wages, greater opportunities, etc.), we must never lose sight that no matter how much any philosophy or movement has to recommend it, every line item of its mission, methods, and mentality must be subject to the Word of God—not vice versa.

For myself, and I know for many others, I ask only enough "liberation" to carry out the clear mandates of Scripture.

# Notes

## CHAPTER ONE

1. Clark Pinnock, "Three Views of the Bible in Contemporary Theology," in *Biblical Authority,* ed. Jack Rogers (Waco, TX: Word Books, 1977), pp. 69–70.
2. Harold Lindsell, "Current Religious Thought, Egalitarianism and Scriptural Infallibility," in *Christianity Today,* March 26, 1976, p. 46.
3. Virginia Mollenkott, "A Conversation with Virginia Mollenkott," *The Other Side,* May-June 1976, p. 25–27.
4. Ibid, p. 30.
5. Virginia Mollenkott and Letha Scanzoni, "Homosexuality: 2 Perspectives," *Daughters of Sarah,* November/December 1977, pp. 6–7.
6. Paul Jewett, *Man as Male and Female* (Grand Rapids: Wm B. Eerdmans Publishing Co., 1975), pp. 136–137.
7. Mollenkott, *Women, Men, and the Bible* (Nashville: Abingdon Press, 1977), p. 103.
8. Scanzoni and Hardesty, *All We're Meant to Be* (Waco, TX: Word Incorporated, 1974), p. 71.
9. Duane Dunham, "Women in the Ministry, Ephesians 5 and Galatians 3," chapel lecture (Portland, OR: Western Conservative Baptist Seminary, 1968), p. 8.
10. Albrecht Oepke, *"gune," Theological Dictionary of the New Testament,* vol. 1, ed. Gerhard Kittel (Grand Rapids: Wm. B. Eerdmans Publishing Co., 1964), p. 785. I would disagree with Oepke that the consumation produces sexless beings, necessarily, or that it is a churse to be a woman.
11. Jewett, *Man as Male and Female,* p. 99.
12. Peter Richardson, "Paul Today: Jews, Slaves, and Women," *Crux* 8 (1971), p. 37.
13. Mollenkott, "A Conversation," p. 26.
14. Scanzoni and Hardesty, *All We're Meant to Be,* p. 28.
15. Umberto Cassuto, *A Commentary on the Book of Genesis,* 2 vols., Part I (Jerusalem: Magnes Press, 1961), p. 130.

## CHAPTER TWO

1. Frederik W. Grosheide, *Commentary on the First Epistle to the Corinthians,* The New International Commentary on the New Testament

(Grand Rapids: Wm. B. Eerdmans Publishing Co., 1953), p. 249.

2. For example Letha Scanzoni and Nancy Hardesty, *all We're Meant to Be* (Waco, TX: Word Books, 1974), pp. 30–31.

3. Markus Barth, *Ephesians 1–3*, The Anchor Bible (Garden City, NY: Doubleday & Co., 1974), pp. 183–92.

4. Stephen Bedale, "The Meaning of ´ in the Pauline Epistles," *Journal of Theological Studies* 5 (1954):215.

5. Catherine Kroeger, "The Classical Concept of 'Head' as 'Source,' *Equal to Serve*, Appendix III, pp. 267–283.

6. Wayne Grudem, "Does *kephale* ('head') Mean 'Source' or 'Authority Over' in Greek Literature? A Survey of 2,336 Examples," appendix 1 in George W. Knight III, *The Role Relationship of Men and Women* (Chicago: Moody Press, 1985), pp. 49–80. In a public debate with feminist Catherine Kroeger, the present author asked for an example of *kephale* as clearly meaning "source" or "origin" and in the singular in extrabiblical literature in the first two centuries of the church era. Dr. Kroeger, though a classicist specializing in Christian literature, was not able to adduce even one, but rather gave an example from the writings of Athanasius.

7. See my article, H. Wayne House, "Should a Woman Prophesy or Preach before Men?," *Bibliotheca Sacra* 145, No. 578(April-June 1988): 145–48.

8. Anthony C. Thiselton, "Semantics and New Testament Interpretation," in *New Testament Interpretation*, ed. I. Howard Marshall (Grand Rapids: Wm. B. Eerdmans Publishing Co., 1977), p. 82.

9. "In view of the importance of the field, Barr and Burres each supports Trier's point that a word has meaning not autonomously or independently but 'only as a part of a whole'(nur als Teil des Ganzen); only within a field *(im Feld)*." Marshall, ed., "Semantics and New Testament Interpretation," *New Testament Interpretation*, p. 83.

10. J. P. Louw, *Semantics of New Testament Greek* (Philadelphia: Fortress Press, 1982), p. 34.

11. Ibid. One writer recently has left behind the argument for "source" and has attempted another one which appears to be less problematic. Walter Liefield argues that *kephale* means the preeminent or prominent one. Though such a meaning is certainly possible [the lexica list this meaning only with things, not persons], the evidence would still seem to favor "authority" or "leader" in most passages in discussion in the Pauline corpus. *Women, Authority & the Bible*, ed. Alvera Mickelsen (Downers Grove, Ill.: InterVarsity Press, 1986), p. 139.

12. H. G. Liddell, George Scott, and Henry Stuart Jones *An Greek-English Lexicon* (Oxford: The Clarendon Press, 1940), p. 945.

13. G. W. Lampe, ed. *Patristic Greek Lexicon* (Oxford: Oxford University Press, 1968), p. 749.

14. *Oxford Classical Dictionary* (1970) p. 59.

15. *Timaeus* 44.D.

16. *Table-Talk* 692.D.11.

17. *Life of Moses* 2.30.
18. Walter Bauer, *A Greek-English Lexicon of the New Testament and Other Early Christian Literature*, trans. by William F. Ardnt, F. Wilbur Gingrich, and Frederick W. Danker (Chicago: The University of Chicago Press, 1957, 1979), p. 430.
19. H. Cremer, *Biblico-Theological Lexicon of New Testament Greek*, trans. by William Urwick (Edinburgh: T & T Clark, 1895), p.
20. Heinrich Schlier, "," *Theological Dictionary of the New Testament*, gen. ed. Gerhard Kittel, trans. and ed. Geoffrey W. Bromiley, Vol 3 (Grand Rapids: Wm. B. Eerdmans Publishing Company, 1965), pp. 674–75.
21. J. H. Thayer, *The Thayer's Greek Lexicon* (Peabody, MA: Hendrickson Publishing Co., 1981).
22. K. Munzer, "Head," *Dictionary of New Testament Theology*, ed. Colin Brown (Grand Rapids: Zondervan Publishing House, 1976), p. 162. Unfortunately, Munzer says that *kephale* in 1 Cor. 11:3 means source or origin. He comes to this conclusion based on a statement by F. F. Bruce (*1 & 2 Corinthians*, [Greenwood, S. C.: The Attic Press, 1971], pl 103) who in turn based his view on the study by Stephen Bedale ("The Meaning of ´ in the Pauline Epistles," 211ff), who in turn never convincingly demonstrated that *kephale* means *source* or *origin* in reference to persons. This is circular argumentation, not proof. K. Munzer, p. 158.
23. Louw, p. 35.
24. See H. Wayne House, "Should a Woman Prophesy or Preach before Men?," *Bibliotheca Sacra* 145, No. 578(April-June 1988): 147–48.
25. Philip Payne, "Libertarian Women in Ephesus: A Response to Douglas J. Moos' Article," '1 Timothy 2:11–15: Meaning and Significance,'" *Trinity Journal* 2 (1981):175.
26. Catherine C. Kroeger, "Ancient heresies and a strange Greek verb," *The Reformed Journal* 29 (March 1979):12–15. This strange interpretation has been well answered by Armin J. Panning, ' - A Word Study', *Wisconsin Lutheran Quarterly* 79 (1981):185–91.
27. Apparently the English translators understood *herrschen* to be the same as *beherrschen*, an uncertain conclusion. If Walter Bauer and Kert and Barbara Alend, *Griechisch-deutaches Worterbruch* (Berlin: Walter de Gruyter, 1988), p. 242.
28. George W. Knight II, " in Reference to Women in 1 Timothy 2 12," *New Testament Studies* 30 (January 1984):143–57
29. Ibid., 150.
30. Leland Edward Wilshire, "The TLG COmputer and Further Reference to in 1 Timothy 2.12," *New Testament Studies* 34 (1988):120–34.
31. See the arguments by William O. Walker, where he discounts, as is standard liberal fare, the Pastorals as having come from the apostle Paul, along with 1 Corinthians 14:34–35, and believes that if 1 Corinthians 11:2–16 is rejected, then all that we have from Paul's hand on the issue of women is Galatians 3:28, viewed as a positive statement on women in the church. He argues that 1 Corinthians is a non-Pauline interpolation

reflecting a anti-feminist group. William O. Walker, "1 Corinthians 11:2–16 and Paul's Views Regarding Women," *Journal of Biblical Literature*, 95, No. 1 (March, 1975): 94–110. For a presentation of Walker's arguments with a detailed rebuttal see H. Wayne House, *An Investigation of Contemporary Feminist Arguments on Paul's Teaching on the Role of Women in the Church* (Th.D. dissertation, Concordia Seminary, St. Louis, 1986), pp. 67–76, and Jerome Murphy-O'Connor, "The Non-Pauline Character of 1 Corinthians 11:2–16?" *Journal of Biblical Literature* 95 (December 1976):619.

32. Gordon D. Fee, *The Epistle to the Corinthians, The New International Commentary on the New Testament*, gen. ed. F. F. Bruce (Grand Rapids: William B. Eerdmans Publishing Company, 1987), pp. 699–700.

33. Ibid, 701–05. Fee's rejection of the Pauline authorship of the pericope is not something new. German scholarship has long considered the text to be a non-Pauline interpolation. Cf. Hans Conzelmann, *I Corinthians* (Hermeneia; Philadelphia: Fortress, 1975), 246; Johannes Weiss, *Der erste Korintherbrief* (Göttingen: Vandenhoeck & Ruprecht, 1970 [1970], 342–43. See the discussion of this in E. Earle Ellis, "The Silenced Wives of Corinth (I Cor. 14:34–35) *New Testament Textual Criticism, Its Significance for Exegesis*, eds. Eldon Jay Epp and Gordon D. Fee (Oxford: Clarendon Press, 1981):213–16. Many scholars also attempt to tie the 14:34–35 pericope to a Pauline school responsible for the Pastorals due to the similar terminology found in 1 Timothy 2:12 and 1 Corinthians 14:34.

34. F. F. Bruce, *1 and 2 Corinthians*, New Century Bible (Greenwood, SC: The Attic Press, 1971), p. 135.

35. Cited by Bruce Metzger, *A Textual Commentary on the Greek New Testament* (New York: United Bible Societies, 1971), p. 565.

36. Cf. Neil Lightfoot, "The Role of Women in Religious Services," *Restoration Quarterly* 19 (1976):131–32, and Hurley, "did Paul Require Veils or the Silence of Women: A Consideration of 1 Cor. 11:2–16 and 1 Cor. 14:33b–36," *Westminster Theological Journal* 35 (1973):216.

37. Jean Héring, *The First Epistle of Saint Paul to the Corinthians* (London: The Epworth Press, 1962), p. 154. The two paragraphs on the textual problem in 1 Corinthians 14:34–35 largely reflect the exact words found in my article, "The Speaking of Women and the Prohibition of the Law," *Bibliotheca Sacra* 145, No. 579 (July-September 1988): 304, f.n. 10, but are given without indentation or quotes.

38. Ellis, 219.

39. Ibid, 219–20.

40. Fee, 702.

41. See the various opinions on the nature of the speaking in verse 34 in House, "The Speaking of Women and the Prohibition of the Law," 305–10.

42. Walter Kaiser, "Paul, Women and the Church," *Worldwide Challenge* (September 1976), 11. [He, it appears, mistakenly says 34b–35 but really means 34a–35].

43. Ibid., 11

44. Ibid., 11–12.
45. Ibid., 12.
46. Fee, 705.
47. Quotation found in Kaiser "Paul, Women and the Church," from citation by Katherine C. Bushnell, *God's Word to Women: One Hundred Bible Studies*, 4th ed., 1930, Lesson 27, ¶205.
48. Walter Kaiser, *Christianity Today Institute* (October 3, 1986):12–I.
49. The first and last brackets are Kaiser's.
50. Thayer's Lexicon, p. 275.
51. Ibid. Italics mine. Examples of this usage given by Thayer are Matt. 7:4 "Or [e] how wilt thou say to thy brother, Let me ull out the mote out of thine eye; and, behold, a beam is in thine own eye?"; Matt. 7:9 Or [e] what man is there of you, whom if his son ask bread, will he give him a stone?; Matt. 12:29 Or [e] else how can one enter into a strong man's house, and spoil his goods, except he first bind the strong man? and then he will spoil his house.; Matt. 16:26 For what is a man profited, if he shall gain the whole world, and lose his own soul? or [e] what shall a man give in exchange for his soul?; Matt. 26:53 [e] Thinkest thou that I cannot now pray to my Father, and he shall presently give me more than twelve legions of angels?; Mark 8:37 Or [e] what shall a man give in exchange for his soul?; Luke 13:4 Or [e] those eighteen, upon whom the tower in Siloam fell, and slew them, think ye that they were sinners above all men that dwelt in Jerusalem?; Luke 14:31 Or [e] what king, going to make war against another king, sitteth not down first, and consulteth whether he be able with ten thousand to meet him that cometh against him with twenty thousand?; Luke 15:8 Either [e] what woman having ten pieces of silver, if she lose one piece, doth not light a candle, and sweetp the house, and seek diligently till she find it?; Rom. 9:21 Hath [or, e] not the potter power over the clay, of the same lump to make one vessel unto honour, and another unto dishonour?; Rom. 14:10 But why dost thou judge thy brother? or [e] why dost thou set at nought thy brother? for we shall all stand before the judgment seat of Christ.; 1 Cor. 6:16 What? [e] know ye not that he which is joined to an harlot is one body? for two, saith he, shall be one flesh.
52. The remainder of the examples by Thayer are: Rom. 3:28 Therefore we conclude that a man is justified by faith apart from the deeds of the law. 29 Or [e] is He the God of the Jews only? Is He not also the God of the Gentiles? Yes, of the Gentiles also.; Rom. 6:23 For the wages of sin is death, but the gift of God is eternal life in Christ Jesus our Lord. 7:1 Or [e] do you not know, brethren (for I speak to those who know the law), that the law has dominion over a man as long as he lives?; Rom. 6:1 What shall we say then? Shall we continue in sin that grace may abound? 2 Certainly not! How shall we who died to sin live any longer in it? 3 Or [e] do you not know that as many of us as were baptized into Christ Jesus were baptized into His death?; Rom. 11:2 God has not cast away His people whom He foreknew. Or [e] do you not know what the Scripture says of Elijah, how he pleads with God against Israel, saying; 1 Cor. 6:8 No, you yourselves do wrong and cheat, and you do these things

to your brethren! 9 Do [e] you not know that the unrighteous will not inherit the kingdom of God? Do not be deceived. Neither fornicators, nor idolaters, nor adulterers, nor homosexuals, nor sodomites,; 1 Cor. 6:18 Flee sexual immorality. Every sin that a man does is outside the body, but he who commits sexual immorality sins against his own body. 19 Or [e] do you not know that your body is the temple of the Holy Spirit who is in you, whom you have from God, and you are not your own?; 1 Cor. 10:21 You cannot drink the cup of the Lord and the cup of demons; you cannot partake of the Lord's table and of the table of demons. 22 Or [e] do we provoke the Lord to jealousy? Are we stronger than He?, 1 Cor. 11:13 Judge among yourselves. Is it proper for a woman to pray to God with her head uncovered? 14 Does [or, e] not even nature itself teach you that if a man has long hair, it is a dishonor to him? [Textus Receptus]; 1 Cor. 14:35 And if they want to learn something, let them ask their own husbands at home; for it is shameful for women to speak in church. 36 What? [e] came the word of God out from you? or came it unto you only?.

53. C. K. Barrett, *A Commentary on the First Epistle to the Corinthians*, Harpers' New Testament Commentaries (New York: Harper & Row, Publishers, 1968), p. 330; William F. Orr and James Arthur Walther, *I Corinthians*, The Anchor Bible (Garden City, NY: Doubleday & Company, 19786), p. 312; F. Godet, *Commentary on St. Paul's First Epistle to the Corinthians*, trans. A. Cusin (Edinburgh: T & T Clark, 1890), p. 309; Heinrich August Wilhelm Meyer, *Critical and Exegetical Hand-Book to the Epistles to the Corinthians* (New York: Funk & Wagnalls, Publishers, 1884), p. 333; F. F. Bruce, *1 and 2 Corinthians*, New Century Bible (Greenwood, SC: The Attic Press, 1971), p. 136.

54. Aída Dina Besançon Spencer, "Eve at Ephesus," *Journal of the Evangelical Theological Society* 17 (Fall 1974):215–22.

55. Ibid., 216.

56. Ibid., 219.

57. Philip Barton Payne, "Libertarian Women in Ephesus: A Response to Douglas J. Moo's Article, '1 Timothy 2:11–15: Meaning and Significance,'" *Trinity Journal* 2 (1981):171.

58. See Moo, "The Interpretation of 1 Timothy 2:11–15: A Rejoinder," *Trinity Journal* 2 (1981):215–21.

59. Payne has argued that the Greek conjunction introducing verse 12, "for" *(gar)*, should not be taken as a causal conjunction but as explanatory. He says, "If *gar* in 1 Tim. 2:13 is explanatory, not illative, the actual *reason* Paul was prohibiting women in Ephesus from teaching is not that Eve was formed after Adam or that she was deceived by Satan, but that some women in Ephesus were (or were on the verge of becoming) *engaged in false teaching*." Payne, "Libertarian Women in Ephesus," 175–77. Payne's claim for an explanatory *gar* is difficult to understand. First, the usage is uncommon (approximately 50 out of more than 1000 occurrences of the conjunction; see Bauer, Arndt, and Gingrich, *A Greek-English Lexicon of the New Testament and Other Early Christian Literature*, p. 151; H. E. Dana and Julius R. Mantey, *A Manual*

*Grammar of the Greek New Testament,* p. 243; and Maximilian Zerwick, *Biblical Greek, §473.), so good reason would need to exist in the context if it is to be preferred over the causal gar.* Second, the move from the command or prohibition to the reason for the command or prohibition is common in Paul (e.g., 1 Tim. 3:13; 4:5, 8, 16; 5:4, 11, 15), and naturally occurs with *gar.* Third, Payne admits Paul is giving a *reason* for his prohibition. The force of the explanatory *gar* is to explicate a previous statement, which verses 13–14 do not. It is better to understand *gar* as introducing the reason paul gave his previous prohibition.

60. Moo, "The Interpretation of 1 Timothy 2:11–15. A Rejoinder,":200.
61. Stephan B. Clark, *Men and Women in Christ* (Ann Arbor, MI: Servant Books, 1980), p. 200.
62. Philip Barton Payne, "O' in 1 Timothy 2:12" (unpublished paper), p. 1.
63. Ibid.
64. Thomas Edgar, "1 Timothy 2:12: An Analysis of Restrictive Interpretation," (unpublished paper), p. 3.
65. Ibid., p. 10. Other examples of this construction are Matthew 6:26; 12:4, 19,; 24:36; Luke 12:27, 33; 16:31; John 1:13, 25; 6:24; 8:11; Acts 7:5; 9:9; 16:21; 17:25; Hebrews 9:12; 1 Peter 2:22; Revelation 5:3; 7:16; 20:4; 21:23.
66. Ibid., p. 10.
67. Matthew 6:20, 28; 13:13; 16:9; Mark 4:22; 8:17; Luke 8:17; John 14:17; Acts 8:21; 16:21; 24:18; Hebrews 10:8; 13:5, 1 Peter 1:8.
68. Edgar, p. 14.
69. Ibid., p. 23.
70. Ibid., p. 24.
71. The section on *oude* is primarily based on a article by me found in H. Wayne House, "The Speaking of Women and the Prohibition of the Law," *Bibliotheca Sacra* 146, No. 579 (July-September 1989): 315–17.

# CHAPTER THREE

1. Some cautions must be given in the interpretation of the status of women in the ancient world: (1) One must be careful not to extrapolate attitudes or practices from one era or culture and place them into another one. Christians vary in the position of time and people differ from one another in the same in the same century in divergent cultures. (2) Making a given author representative of an entire culture can be a mistake. He may reflect the general mood, or on the other hand, his view may be personal bias or the bias of a subculture. Authors often differ among themselves. (3) In interpreting cultural positions one must be careful not to assume that privileges or responsibilities of one rank in a society are those of other ranks or classes. (4) The laws of a given society are not necessarily strictly enforced, nor are they indicative of the familiar attitude between spouses, parents, and children, whose love for one another are of a much higher plane. (5) When one reads an author on the

subject of values in a culture, one must be certain to discern properly the intention for his presentation in order to interpret him correctly. He may, at times, be overstressing this point (as in a court trial, or in a comedy).

2. Eugenia Leonard, "St. Paul on the Status of Women," *Catholic Biblical Quarterly* 12 (July 1950):312.

3. Sarah Pomeroy, *Goddesses, Whores, Wives, and Slaves* (New York: Schocken Books, 1975), pp. 30–31.

4. W. K. Lacey, *The Family in Classical Greece* (Ithaca: Cornell University Press, 1968), p. 153.

5. Hesiod, *Works and Days* 57–94.

6. *Herodotus* 1. 196.

7. Plato, *Republic* 5. 451, 455C–456B.

8. Plato, *The Symposium*, trans. W. Hamilton (Harmonds-worth: Penguin Books, 1951), p. 12.

9. Plato, *Laws* 3. 694–695a; cf. also *Republic* 8.849 cd, where mothers are viewed as a threat to the development of the character of their sons.

10. Evelyn and Frank Stagg, *Woman in the World of Jesus* (Philadelphia: The Westminster Press, 1978), p. 75.

11. Plato, *Timaeus* 90C, cited by Stagg, p. 75. Reincarnation is in view here.

12. Aristotle, *Politics* 1. 5. 2.

13. Aristotle, *Politics* 1. 12.

14. Charles C. Ryrie, *The Place of Women in the Church* (Chicago: Moody Press, 1958), pp. 2–3.

15. *Thucydides* 2. 45. 2, cited by Ryrie, p. 4.

16. Xenophon, *Oeconomicus* 7. 18; cf. Lacey p. 171 on the various kinds of economic endeavor of poor women and citizen women.

17. Pomeroy, p. 36.

18. Plutarch, Life of Lycurgus 14–16, excerpts found in Mary R. Lefkowitz and Maureen B. Fant, *Women in Greece and Rome* (Toronto: Samuel-Stevens, 1977), pp. 52–54.

19. Plutarch, *Sayings of Spartan Women* 240–242, excerpts found in Lefkowitz and Fant, p. 53.

20. Letha Scanzoni and Nancy Hardesty, *All We're Meant to Be* (Waco, TX: Word Books, 1974), p. 51.

21. Plutarch, *Pericles* 24. 4. 2. 5. 2, cited by James Donaldson, *Woman; her Position and Influence in Ancient Greece and Rome, and Among the Early Christians* (New York: Gordon Press, 1973 reprint), pp. 60–66.

22. Lacey, p. 174.

23. E. M. Blaiklock, *From Prison to Rome—Letters to the Philippians and Philemon* (Grand Rapids: Zondervan Publishing House, 1964), p. 47.

24. Ryrie, pp. 4–5.

25. Stagg, p. 60.

26. See examples of Sappho's poetry in Lefkowitz and Fant, pp. 3–6.

27. Stagg, pp. 58–62.

28. Jerome Carcopino, *Daily Life in Ancient Rome* (New Haven: Yale University Press, 1940), p. 77.

29. Ibid.
30. Pomeroy, p. 150.
31. Ibid., p. 151.
32. Ibid., p. 150.
33. Ibid., p. 152.
34. E. R. Boak, *A History of Rome to 565 A.D.*, 3rd ed. (New York: The Macmillan Company, 1947), p. 89.
35. Stagg, p. 82.
36. Dio Chrysostom, *Tarsica prior Orat.* 33. 408M, cited from Donaldson, p. 150.
37. Constance F. Parvey, "The Theology and Leadership of Women in the New Testament," in *Religion and Sexism*, ed. Rosemary Radford Ruether (New York: Simon and Schuster, 2974), pp. 118–19.
38. Pomeroy, p. 151.
39. Ibid.
40. Ibid.
41. Carcopino, p. 84.
42. S. A. Cook, F. E. Adcock, M. P. Charlesworth, gen. eds., *The Cambridge Ancient History,* vol. 11: *The Imperial Peace,* A.D. 70–192 (Cambridge: University Press, 1936), p. 694. However, Musonius Rufus also taught that sexual intercourse is only for procreation, and pursuit of mere pleasure is wrong and perverse even inside marriage. Ibid.
43. See Pomeroy for discussion, pp. 205–226. Religion was not always advantageous to women, e.g. the worship of Bacchus, dominated by women, became so degraded that it was declared illegal in 181 B.C., and many of its adherents were put to death. Ryrie, p. 7.
44. The gradual rising of women to a more nearly equal status with men in Roman society was not without criticism, nor was all the criticism without justification. Even Plautus, of the Republican era, writes in *The Comedy of Asses* of a wife who henpecked her husband. "The husband Demaenetus myself! Gave up my authority for a dowry!" (1. 16–22), cited by Stagg, p. 81. Such a portrayal would be understood by the audience only if such happened in reality. Cato the Elder (234–149 B.C.) rejected the change in the legal status of wives, asserting that women would gradually release themselves from bonds one by one if the lawmakers were not careful so as to be equals and ultimately superiors of men. Parvey, p. 120.
45. Carcopino, p. 92, comments, "The feminism which triumphed in imperial times brought more in its train than advantage and superiority. By copying men too closely the Roman women succeeded more rapidly in emulating man's vices than in acquiring his strength."
46. Seneca, *De Beneficiis* 3. 16. 2.
47. Carcopino, p. 93. The low birthrate that existed in the time of the Empire may have been because of the *laissez faire* attitude expressed in this statement, translated by author from the Latin.
48. Cited by Stagg, p. 50.
49. Ryric, p. 8.

50. *The Authorized Daily Prayer Book* (London: Valentine and Co., 1947), p. 21.
51. Ibid.
52. Joseph Bonsirven, *Palestinian Judaism in the Time of Jesus Christ*, trans. William Wolf (New York: Holt, Rinehart and Winston, 1964), p. 100.
53. *Testament of Reuben* 3.10.
54. Philo, *Hypothetica* 11. 14.
55. Stagg, p. 38.
56. Philo, *De Cherubim* 40–52.
57. Stagg, p. 41.
58. Josephus, *Antiquities of the Jews* 2. 4. 5.
59. Josephus, *Antiquities* 17. 5. 6.
60. She could petition the courts to have her husband divorce her, however.
61. Leonard, p. 312.
62. Stagg, p. 43.
63. Parvey, p. 120.
64. Ryrie, pp. 10–11.
65. Ibid., p. 11. Kohler says that in later Judaism the woman was not counted as a member of the religious community. Kaufmann Kohler, *Jewish Theology* (New York: KTAV Publishing House, Inc., 1968), p. 472.
66. Josephus, *Apion* 2, 8, cited by Stagg, p. 48.
67. Louis M. Epstein, *Sex Laws and Customs in Jerusalem* (New York: KTAV Publishing House, Inc., 1967), p. 78.

## CHAPTER FOUR

1. Eugenia Leonard, "St. Paul on the Status of Women," *Catholic Biblical Quarterly* 12 (July 1950): 312. An exception is found in Musonius Rufus discussed in chapter three.
2. Joseph Holzner, *Paul of Tarsus* (St. Louis: Herder Book Co., 1945), p. 239.

## CHAPTER FIVE

1. Attitudes toward women varied, and since the world was primarily a man's world the shining personalities of noble women of this era are hidden from view. The exceptions are the women martyrs such as the slave girl Blandina at Lyons and the noble Perpetua with the slave girl Felicitas. There are various references to women occupying positions like virgin, widow, or deaconess in the literature of the church but only in terms of class and not as individuals. Everett Ferguson, *Early Christians Speak* (Austin, Tex.: Sweet Publishing Company, 1971), p. 232. Donaldson reacts to this situation rather sarcastically: "Every honour was heaped after death on the woman who thus suffered for Christ's sake, and their ashes and other relics were supposed to exercise a sanctifying

and miraculous influence; but during their lives it was their duty to stay home and manage the affairs of their household and not meddle in teaching or any spiritual function." James Donaldson, *Woman: Her Positioon and Influence in Ancient Greece and Rome, and Among the Early Christians* (New York: Gordon Press, 1973), p. 157.

2. Fritz Zerbst, *The Office of Woman in the Church* (St. Louis: Concordia Publishing House, 1955), p. 82.

3. Tatian, *To the Greeks* 33. 13–15.

4. Clement of Alexandria, *Stromata* 4. 8. 29–31.

5. *Stromata.* 4. 8. 33–38.

6. Clement of Alexandria, "Paedagogus," I, 4 *Ante-Nicene Fathers*, vol. 2 (Grand Rapids: Wm. B. Eerdmans Publishing Company, 1962), p. 211; Elsewhere he says " 'Man' here is a common noun not restricted to male or female. The very name 'mankind' is a name common to both men and women." Cited by Zerbst, p. 93; cf. L. Zscharnack, *Der Dienst der Frau in den ersten Jahrhunderten der christlichen Kirche* (Gottingen, 1902), p. 13.

7. Zerbst, *The Office of Woman in the Church*, p. 93.

8. Ibid; a balanced view on Tertullian if found in F. F. Church, "Sex and Salvation in Tertullian," *Harvard Theological Review* 68 (April 1975):83–101.

9. Pseudo-Clementine, *Homilies* 1.27, trans. Thomas Smith, *Ante-Nicene Fathers*, vol. 8, p. 243.

10. Tertullian, *On the Apparal of Women* 1. 1, trans. S. Thelwall, *Ante-Nicene Fathers*, vol. 4, p. 14.

11. Examples of these are the *Didache*, the *Didascalia Apostolorum*, the *Apostolic Tradition*, the *Apostolic Church Order*, and the late fourth-century *Apostolic Constitutions*.

12. Tertullian, *Adversus Marcion* 5. 8. 11, ed. and trans. Ernest Evans, Oxford Early Christian Texts (Oxford: At the Clarendon Press, 1972), p. 560.

13. Cf. Jean Danielou, *The Ministry of Women in the Early Church* (Leighton Buzzard: The Faith Press, 1961), p. 11.

14. Origen, *Jes. hom.* 6, cited by Zerbst, p. 90.

15. J. V. Bartlet, "Fragments of the *Didascalia Apostolorum* in Greek," *The Journal of Theological Studies* 18 (July 1917): 307. This fragment corresponds to the later *Apostolic Constitutions* iii 5.6–6.4. Bartlet, 301–309; cf. the *a fortiori* argument regarding teaching and the priesthood: "But if we have not permitted them [women] to teach, how will any one allow them, contrary to nature, to perform the office of a priest? For this is one of the ignorant practices of the atheism of the Greeks (Gentiles) to appoint priestesses to the female deities." *Apostolic Constitutions* iii.c.ix cited by Donaldson, p. 163. Tertullian has similar sentiment, "It is not permitted to a woman to speak in the church; but neither to teach, nor to baptize, nor to offer, nor to claim to herself any manly office, not to mention the sacerdotal office." *De virginibus velandis* 9.2; also in *De Baptismo*, he reiterates this theme: "How are we to believe that he [Paul] gave to a female the power to teach and baptize

when he did not permit a woman even to learn with overboldness [*constanter*]. 'Let them be silent,' he says, 'and at home consult their own husbands.'" *De Baptismo* 17. 26–29.

16. Donaldson, p. 165.

17. Ibid.

18. *Didache.* 10:7. This text connects prophecy and thanks, an observation made in chapter 4, p. 67 in the discussion on 1 Corinthians 11.

19. Zerbst, p. 85.

20. Origen, *Fragments on 1 Corinthians* 74, cited by Gryson, pp. 28–29; cf. C.H. Turner, "Notes on the Text of Origen's Commentary on 1 Corinthians," *Journal of Theological Studies* 10 (1909): 270–76.

21. Roger Gryson, *The Ministry of Women in the Early Church*, trans. Jean Laporte and Mary Louise Hall (Collegeville, Minn.: The Liturgical Press, 1976), p. 15.

22. Ibid.

23. Elaine Pagels, *The Gnostic Gospels* (New York: Random House, 1979), p. 65.

24. Zerbst, p. 84.

25. Tertullian, *De Praescr.* 41, cited by Pagels p. 60.

26. Hippolytus, Ref. 5.6, cited by Pagels, p. 49.

27. Pagels, pp. 49–50.

28. *The Apocryphon of John* 2.1, 2, trans. by Frederik Wisse, *The Nag Hammadi Library*, gen. ed. James Robinson (New York: Harper & Row, Publishers, 1977), p. 99.

29. Pagels, pp. 51–52.

30. *The Gospel of Thomas* 2. 49, 35–50, 1, trans. by Thomas O. Lambdin, *The Nag Hammadi Library*. pp. 128–129.

31. Pagels, pp. 60–61.

32. Zerbst, p. 85.

33. Polycarp, *Epistle to the Philippians* 4.

34. Ignatius, *Epistle to the Smyrnaeans* 13, trans. J. B. Lightfoot, *The Apostolic Fathers* (Grand Rapids: Baker Book House, 1956), p. 85.

35. For a discussion of the ungodly widows see William Hendriksen, *Exposition of the Pastoral Epistles, New Testament Commentary* (Grand Rapids: Baker Book House, 1967), p. 170.

36. Hendriksen says the idea the "let these first learn" refers to the widows rather than the children is clearly erroneous. Note the plural verb whereas widow is singular. "That is their first religious (cf. Acts 17:23) duty toward those who brought them up. They should strive to make a *real return* (acc. pl. of amoibe, plural of intensity) for all the care that was so slovingly bestowed upon them. Note, 'Let these first *learn*' this lesson. By nature children are often disinclined to provide for their needy parents. . . . But even if it means self-denial, this lesson must be learned. It is certainly implied in the fifth commandment." Hendriksen, pp. 168–169.

37. This is a technical term meaning registration. Martin Dibelius and Hans Conzelmann, *The Pastoral Epistles, Hermeneia Series* (Philadelphia: Fortress Press, 1972), p. 75.

38. Everett Ferguson, "Widows and the church," *Firm Foundation* (December 8, 1981): 6; contra Daniélou, pp. 13–14: "Here the stress is laid on the ascetic and contemplative side of the life the widows lead, rather than on their functions within the community."
39. Hendriksen says that verse 10 indicates some of the enrolled widows may have been well-to-do. Hendriksen, p. 173.
40. R. St. John Parry, *The Pastoral Epistles.* (Cambridge: At the University Press, 1920), p. 31.
41. Homer Kent, *The Pastoral Epistles* (Chicago: Moody Press, 1958), pp. 172–174.
42. Ferguson, "Widows and the Church," 6.
43. Dix, p. 11.
44. Daniélou, p. 18.
45. *Didascalia* 3. 6. 1–2; Bartlet, pp. 304–305; Daniélou, pp. 18–19; Zerbst, p. 89.
46. *Didascalia* 3. 9. 1–3, cited by Gryson, p. 38.
47. *The Apostolic Tradition of Hyppolytus* 10, cited Dix p. 20. The brackets are mine.
48. *De pudicitia* 13.7, cited by Gryson, p. 21; on *ordo* see P. van Beneden "Ordo, Ueber den Ursprung einer kirchlichen Terminologie," in *Vigiliae christianae* 23 (1969):161–76.
49. Clement of Alexandria, *Pedagogue* 3. 12, *Ante-Nicene Fathers,* vol. 2, p. 294.
50. *Homilies on Luke* 17, cited by Gryson, p. 26.
51. Grysons, ps. 24; Ferguson in defining the terminology of the *Apostolic Constitutions,* a Syrian book akin to the *Didascalia,* and written in the fourth century in the region of Antioch, distinguishes *cheirontonia* from *kathistanai. Cheirontonia* is used of formal appointment whereas *kathistanai* can be used for appointment of church functionaries, as in the installation of bishops, ordination of deacons, or the enrollment of widows. But widows did not receive the "laying on of hands." This latter rite was "not the equivalent of *cheirontonia,* but express [sic] the visible sign of which *cheirontonia* is the whole." Everett Ferguson, "Ordination in the Ancient Church: An Examination of the Tehological and Constitutional Motifs in the Light of Biblical and Gentile Sources" (Ph.D. dissertation, Harvard University, 1959), 254–255, 266.
52. Gryson, p. 36, 41; Contra, Donaldson, p. 163.
53. Daniélou, pp. 19–20, 24.
54. Scroggs in reference to Corinth and Lane in reference to Ephesus present cases that these churches were heavily influenced by an over-realized eschatology that deemphaized marriage since the resurrection of Christ brought in the "age to come." Robin Scroggs, "Paul and the Eschatological Woman," *Journal of the American Association of Religion* 40 (1972): 283–303; W. L. Lane, "I Tim. iv.1–3. An Early Instance of Over-realized Eschatology?" *New Testament Studies* 11 (1964–1965), 165–67.
55. Sister M. Rosamond Nugent, *Portrait of the Consecrated Woman in Greek Christian Literature of the First Four Centuries,* no. 64 of Pa-

tristic Studies (Washington, D.C.: The Catholic University of America Press, 1941), pp. 3–4.
56. *Acts of Paul and Thecla* 2. 3–9.
57. Howe, p. 36.
58. *De virginibus velandis* 9. 3–4; cf. Gryson, p. 22.
59. Ignatius of Antioch, *Epistle to Smyrneans* 13. 1.
60. Theodor Zahn, *Ignatius von Antiochien*, pp. 336, 585, cited by Gryson, p. 13.
61. Gryson, p. 13.
62. Daniélou, p. 20.
63. Pliny the Younger, *Letters to Trajan* 2. 10, 96, 8; cf. Karl Hermann Schelkle, *The Spirit and the Bride* (Collegeville, Minn.: The Liturgical Press, 1979), p. 158.
64. Since Pliny was the governor of Bithynia, a Greek speaking province of Asia Minor, one may properly assume that he translated a Greek term into Latin. Gryson, p. 130.
65. Ignatius had used the imagery of the bishop as the Father, and the deacon as Christ, and the presbyters as the apostles, but now the *Didascalia* has gone further with the deaconess as the Holy Spirit. Gryson, p. 41.
66. *Didascalia* 3. 12. 1–13. 1, cited by Gryson p. 40–41.
67. Zerbst, pp. 89–90.
68. Ibid., p. 89.
69. Ibid., p. 22.
70. Prohl, p. 75.
71. Paul K. Jewett, *The Ordination of Women* (Grand Rapids: William B. Eerdmans Publishing Company, 1980), p. 73.
72. Ibid.; Zerbst, pp. 91–92.

# CHAPTER SIX

1. Form critical studies by Wayne A. Meeks ("The Image of the Androgyne: Some Uses of a Symbol in Earliest Christianity," *Harvard Review* 13 [1973–74]: 180–83), Robin Scroggs, ("Paul and the Eschatological Woman," *Journal of the American Academy of Religion* 40 [1972]:291–93), Heinrich Schlier, (*Der Brief an die Galater*, pp. 174–75), and Jurgen Becker, (*Der Brief an die Galater* [Göttingen: Vandenhoeck und Ruprecht, 1976], p. 45–46) suggest that Galatians 3:26–28 may have been cited from a baptismal formula by the Apostle Paul. Two other Pauline passages, 1 Corinthians 12:12–13 and Colossians 3:9–11, contain a similar sequence of thought: baptism into one body, uniting pairs of opposites, and stress on unity in Christ. (Note the similarities of the texts: Galatians 3:26–28; Colossians 3:10–11; 1 Corinthians 12:13). These three may be reflective of early baptismal formulas that Paul usedto develop his unity theme in these three passages. (See the writer's "An Investigation of Contemporary Feminist Arguments, pp. 27–31, for further discussion of this). Whether Paul was quoting or adapting an ear-

lier baptismal formula in no way affects the meaning or impact of his use of it in Galatians 3:28. He is clearly reflecting a matrix of relationships well recognized in the ancient world as being at opposite poles in the social context, one that for Paul in no way hinders union around the new Man, Christ Jesus: Cf. also Vernon H. Neufeld, *The Earliest Christian Confessions* (Grand Rapids: Wm. B. Eerdmans Publishing Co., 1963), p. 62; for an example in Greek literature see Ben Witherington III, "Rite and Rights for Women," *New Testament Studies* 27 (1981):594.

2. Paul K. Kewett, *Man as Male and Female* (Grand Rapids: Wm. B. Eerdmans Publishing Co., 1975), p. 142.

3. Ibid. See also Robert Jewett, "The Sexual Liberation of the Apostle Paul," (paper presented at the 1978 meeting of the Society of Biblical Literature, New Orleans, November, 1978), p. 13. Madeleine Boucher describes the significance of Galatians 3:28 in less optimistic terms. "Some Unexplored Parallels to 1 Cor. 11, 11–12 and Gal. 3,28, the New Testament on the Role of Women," *Catholic Biblical Quarterly* 31 (January 1969):50–60.

4. Robin Scroggs, "Women in the NT," *The Interpreter's Dictionary of the Bible,* Supplementary Volume (Nashville: Abingdon Press, 1976), p. 966.

5. Stendahl, *The Bible and the Role of Women,* pp. 33–34. Regarding the first assumption he has argued that in Galatians 3:28 Paul has brought a destruction of the dichotomy between social order and *coram Deo.* He directs the theological statement of this passage against the former order of creation, in which he says woman is given a subordinate function in society and church. He believes that in Galatians 3:28 Paul goes beyond the prevailing view and practice of the New Testament church. Concerning the second assumption Stendahl argues that all three of the pairs in Galatians 3:28 are to be equally implemented in the life and structure of the church. This biblical text is the key to this implementation of social equality for women today. Even as the idea found in this passage was instrumental in the release of slaves in the 19th century, so few today, he says, "would confine the implications of 'neither slave nor free' to an attitude of the heart, apart from social structure and legislation" Ibid.

6. Umberto Cassuto gives the sense of the poetry in verse 27: "At this point the text assumes a more exalted tone and becomes poetic (*Commentary on the Book of Genesis. Part I From Adam to Noah,* trans. Israel Abrahams (Jerusalem: Magnes Press, 1961), p. 57). See this writer's "An Investigation of Contemporary Feminist Arguments," pp. 41–55, for further discussion of Genesis 1:26–28 and various feminist arguments on the passage.

7. Walther Eichrodt, *Theologie des alten Testaments,* Teil II; *Gott und Welt* (Göttingen: Vandenhoeck and Ruprecht, 1961), p. 100.

8. John J. Davis, "Some Reflections on Galatians 3:28, Sexual Roles, and Biblical Hermeneutics," *Journal of the Evangelical Theological Society* 19, (Summer 1976):202–3.

9. The lack of the article with each pair in verse 28 probably indicates character or quality.

10. Scroggs, *Women in the NT,* p. 966.

11. Witherington makes an interesting observation that Paul's use of eil" rather than neuter e{n, for Christ is a "reaffirmation of Paul's view of male headship" ("Rite and Rights for Women," p. 603, n. 22.

12. Paul Jewett, Mollenkott, Scanzoni and Hardesty—some of the major contemporary "evangelical" feminists seem to have borrowed their hermeneutical procedure from Stendahl and the new hermeneutic. For an interaction with Stendahl's selectivity in using Galatians as his model over against other Pauline texts, see Hans C. Cavallin, "Demythologising the Liberal Illusion," in *Why Not? Priesthood and the Ministry of Women,* p. 88.

## CHAPTER SEVEN

1. See views of angels in J. A. Fitzmyer, "A Feature of Qumran Angelology and the Angels of 1 Cor. 11:10," *New Testament Studies* Vol. 4 (1957–58):48–58.

2. Grosheide relates this authority structure to the recreation order in Christ, not the original creation, but it seems that the latter is also true—11:8f. Frederik Willem Grosheide, *Commentary on the First Epistle to the Corinthians, The New International Commentary on the New Testament* (Grand Rapids: Wm. B. Eerdmans Publishing Company, 1953), p. 249. Such a hierarchical view of the passage does not appear to be in view. It would be graphed as follows:

Gilbert Bilezikian argues that the verse depicts the creation of man, the subsequent formation of woman and lastly the birth of Christ. Gilbert Bilezikian, *Beyond Sexual Roles* (Grand Rapids: Baker Book House, 1986), pp. 38–39. The chronological view, as he calls it, does not explain why Christ in the first caluse is the divine Christ, while Christ in the last clause is the human Christ Moreover, there appears to be an assumption with the view that *kephale* carries the idea of source or origin, which, contrary to much "word magic" cannot be sustained in the writings of Paul, especially in this passage. He graphs his perspective as follows:

### Chronological View

| Christ/man | man/woman | God/Christ |
|---|---|---|
| (creation of man) first | (formation of woman) second | (birth of Christ) third |

3. This repetitive feature, known as "climax," is common in Greek, in which the key word of the preceding comment is used in the following. F. Blass, A. Debrunner, and Robert W. Funk, *A Greek Grammar of the*

*New Testament and Other Early Christian Literature* (Chicago: The University of Chiago Press, 1961), p. 261, para. 493 (3). Blass, Debrunner and Funk, however, in contrast to this author, do not believe that 1 Corinthians 11:3 is an example of "climax."

4. See chapter 2, footnotes 10 & 11 w/their accompanying text.

5. Murphy-O'Connor believes that Christ "designates not the Risen Lord but the community of believers (e.g. 1 Cor. 12:12)." Murphy-O'Connor, 617. The suggestion is intriging: it would tightly unite verse 3 and 16 together. But Paul's discussion does not lend itself to this idea in verses 2–16. As well, his normal terms of identification are one like "in Christ" (e.g. 11:11) or body of Christ.

6. Morna Hooker, "Authority on Her Head: An Examination of 1 Cor. 11:10," *New Testament Studies* Vol. 10 (July 1964):410.

7. Contra. Noel Weeks, "Of Silence and Head Covering," *Westminster Theological Journal*, Vol. 35 (Fall 1972):21–27.

8. The rabbis added four more, namely, Sarah, Hannah, Abigail, and Esther, though the rabbis do not list Noadiah. The LXX has Noadiah as a prophet, not prophetess. A. Isaksson, *Marriage and Ministry in the New Temple*, trans. by Neil Tomkinson and Jean Gray (Lund: C. W. K. Gleerup, 1965), p. 157, 59.

9. Palma argues that the age of the Spirit fulfills what Moses had desired, that is, that all God's people might be prophets. He, then, believes that there is a clear distinction between the "office" of prophet and the "function" of prophet. Anthony Palma, "Tongues and Prophecy—A Comparative Study in Charismata" (STM thesis, Concordia Seminary, St. Louis, 1966), pp. 5–9.

10. Noel Weeks (21–27) argues that the apostle is really against the women praying and prophesying. Paul, he says, sought to show them the impropriety of such action by *reductio ad absurdum:* if woman is going to function in a male role she should be shaved. But since this is absurd, it is clear she should not prophesy.

11. Daniélou, *Ministry of Women in the Church*, pp. 10–11.

12. Daniélou says, "One thing is certain, women are not allowed to teach in the Christian congregation. . . But the role of the prophet in the Church is not primarily that of giving instruction: this is the duty of the teacher. The prophetic role is essentially concerned with prayer."

The *Didache* reveals that the prophet was linked with giving of thanks (Did. 10:7): "Let the prophets give thanks as they will"). It may be that the Old Testament office of prophet, which included teaching, exhortation, revelation, and prayer, has been divided in the New Age with, for example, teacher and prophet functining in different spheres. Women may have been allowed the prophetic sphere of one who prays but not that of teacher, or giver of revelation. Jean Danielou, *The Ministry of Women in the Early Church*, trans. by Glyn Simon (Leighton Buzzard: The Faith Press, 1961), pp. 10–11.

13. Earl Radmacher, "The Pre-Eminence of Preaching," Western Communicator, (Fall 1982):2.

14. Oscar Cullmann, *Early Christian Worship*, trans. A. Stewart Todd

and James B. Torrance (Chicago: Henry Regnery Company, 1953), p. 20, cited by Anthony David Palma, "Tongues and Prophecy—A Comparative Study in Charismata," (STM thesis, Concordia Seminary, St. Louis, 1966), pp. 56–57. See also Ernest Best, "Prophets and Preachers," *Scottish Journal of Theology,* 12 June 1959):150 and R. B. Y. Scott, "Is Preaching Prophecy?" *Canadian Journal of Theology,* 1 (April 1955):16. Wayne Grudem has offered a new perspective on prophetic revelation in the New Testament. He argues that the revelation is similar to an impression from God upon which the prophet acts by word or deed. The prophetic word, however, being subject to misunderstanding by the prophet, is subject to evaluation by the other prophets. This would indicate that it is not infallible as is the Scriptures. Wayne Grudem, "Prophecy—Yes, But Teaching—No: Paul's Consistent Advocacy of Women's Participation without Governing Authority," (unpublished paper), pp. 1–22.

15. Harold Hoehner, "The Purpose of Tongues in 1 Corinthians 14:20–25," *Walvoord: A Tribute* (Chicago: Moody Press, 1982), pp. 56–57.

16. F. W. Grosheide, *Commentary on the First Epistle to the Corinthians,* The New International Commentary (Grand Rapids: Wm. B. Eerdmans Publishing Co., 1953), p. 287. See a similar opinion by Gerhard Friedrich in subtopic "Evangelium und Prophetie" in his article "Propheten and Prophezeien im Neuen Testament," *Theologisches Woerterbuch zum Neuen Testament,* ed. Gerhard Friedrich (Stuttgart: W. Kohlhammer, 1959), VI:856–57.

17. The majority of commentators and authors with whom this writer is acquainted see verses 2–16 in the context of public worship. A few, however, have demurred from this view. Alexander, after he states that verses 17–34 certainly concern church worship, asserts, "On the contrary, verses 21–6 appear to be an outgrowth of the previous discussion on Christian freedom and not related to the aspect of church worship." Ralph Alexander, "An Exegetical Presentation on 1 Corinthians 11:2–16 and 1 Timothy 2:8–15," p. 4. Against this view is A. Isaksson, *Marriage and Ministry in the New Temple,* pp. 155–57.

18. Does *aner* and *gune* refer to the husband and wife, man and wife, or both? Isaksson provides several reasons that the terms refer to husband and wife: (1) The mention of the *gune* as the *doxa* of the *aner* is parallel to a Jewish tomb in Rome with a similar description, namely, *he doxa Sophroniou Lukilla eulogemene;* (2) the wife is the husband's glory *(cbd)* in the Old Testament and rabbinical thought; (3) The *plen* of verse 11 indicates that husband and wife are meant and should not be taken as an adversative but as a concluding statement; neither husband nor wife are exempt from paying proper respect to the other; (4) verse 12 shows that even as the church are not to annull the relationship of man and woman in marriage, neither is it to annull the sexual differences between man and woman. A.Isaksson, *Marriage and Ministry in the New Temple,* p. 175. In contrast to Isaksson, Alexander gives seven reasons why *aner* and *gune* should be taken as man and woman: (1) Man and woman

would be the normal uses of the Greek terms; (2) the word *aner* is the popular term used to translate *ish* in the LXX; (3) verse 3 qualifies *andros* with the adjective "every," which would tend to indicate all men are in view, not just husbands; (4) the anarthrous *gunaikos* emphasizes the nature of a woman in verse 3. If wife were intended, the article would be more appropriate to specify *the* wife of the man; (5) since verses 4 and 5 use the word *pas* when speaking of man and woman praying and prophesying, it would seem that men and woman in general are intended, not husbands and wives. "What would unmarrieds do when they pray and prophesy?;" (6) the creation is the basis for the regulations in verses 7–11. This would tend to stress men and women in general. Also, since verses 11–12 speak of the mutual interdependence of the man and woman—it would be illogical to consider the husband coming into being through the wife and vice versa—the sense of man and woman seems to be maintained; (7) verses 13–16 argue from nature and so apparently concern man and woman. Ralph Alexander, "An Exegetical Presentation on 1 Corinthians 11:2–16 and 1 Timothy 2:8–15," pp. 5–6. Neither of these positions is totally correct. The text seems to lean toward a general sense of man and woman. Certainly man rather than husband is intended in verse 4 because prophesying was not reserved for husbands, and the mention of the interdependence of man and woman in verses 8 and 9 strongly suggests that Alexander, rather than Isaksson, has the right idea. The concept of husband, however, seems implied in verses 4–5 with the shaming of the respective heads, the ones mentioned in verse 3. There seems to be a *double entendre* or *Stichwort*, as is suggested by Bruce Waltke, so that both may be intended. Bruce Waltke, "I Corinthians 11:2–16: An Interpretation," *Bibliotheca Sacra* 135 (Jan-Mar 1978):51. The clarification of Zerbst sheds light on the problem:

One may perhaps say, therefore, that every word concerning marriage is at the same time a word concerning the relationships between men and women in general, and vice versa, that every declaration concerning the relationship between the sexes in general is decisive also for marriage. This fact explains the characteristic indefiniteness of 1 Cor. 11, which in one place speaks of men and women in general and in another place of married people in particular. Fritz Zerbst, *The Office of Women in the Church*, p. 34.

Thus the apostle appears to speak in general terms that may apply to either married or unmarried persons. The essential nature of males and females is the same regardless, as is the commands and intentions of God for them. They are equally sexual beings to fulfill the creation mandate to procreate; they are equally relational and intelligent beings to dominate the earth, with the man providing the leadership; and they are equally spiritual beings to worship their Creator.

19. A. Isaksson, *Marriage and Ministry in the New Temple*, trans. by Neil Tomkinson and Jean Gray (Lund. C. W. K. Gleerup, 1965), p. 182. He thinks that the conduct of the prophetesses was to them a conveyance of the image of the bride of Christ prepared for His coming.

20. James Hurley, "Did Paul Require Veils or the Silence of Women: A Consideration of 1 Cor. 11:2–16 and 1 Cor. 14:33b–36," p. 211.
21. Just exactly what the symbol of submission Paul desired is difficult to determine and is not ultimately significant for the present study. Whatever it may have been several points are clear: (1) The symbol carried a great importance because "the people of Paul's day felt much more keenly than do people of our day that the outward demeanor of a person is an expression of inner life, specifically, of his religious convictions and moral attitude" Fritz Zerbst, *The Office of Women in the Church*, p. 40; (2) the symbol carried the significance in the Christian assembly of conveying the recognition on the part of men and women alike of the submission of woman to man—wife to husband—inaugurated in the creation narratives. When they perform a charismatic activity usually reserved for men they are to indicate they are still in submission; (3) only prophetesses are in view in 1 Corinthians 11:2–16: no mention is made of women having this requirement when in a passive role at the meeting; (4) the practice is not reflective of a merely local custom since Paul appeals to the practice of all the churches (v. 16); his admonitions are based on theology, namely, (a) women are the glory of men (v. 7), (b) men have priority over women because of creation (vv. 8–9), they are to maintain this authority *(exousia)* symbol because of the angles (v. 10), and because it is in agreement with nature (creation) (v. 14). On the meaning of *exousia* see Morna Hooker, "Authority on Her Head: An Examination of 1 Cor. 11:10," and E. E. Kellett, "A Note on 'Power on the Head,'" *Expository Times*, 23 (1911/12):39. On the meaning of *dia tous angelous* see J. A. Fitzmyer, "A Feature of Qumran Angelology and the Angels of 1 Cor. 11:10," *New Testament Studies*, 4 (1957–58):48–58, and W. Foerster, "Zu 1 Cor. 11:10," *Zeitschrift für die Neutestamentliche Wissenschaft* 30 (1931):185–86.
22. See the argument of Ralph Alexander, An Exegetical Presentation on 1 Corinthians 11:2–16 and 1 Timothy 2:8–15," p. 8.
23. Otto Flender, "Image," *The New International Dictionary of New Testament Theology*, Vol. 2, ed. by Colin Brown (Grand Rapids: Zondervan Publishing House, 1978), pp. 286–88.
24. Sverre Aalen, "Glory," *The New International Dictionary of New Testament Theology*, Vol. 2, pp. 44–46; Walter Bauer, *A Greek-English Lexicon of the New Testament and Other Early Christian Literature*, trans. by William F. Arndt, and F. Wilbur Gingrich (Chicago: The University of Chicago Press, 1957).
25. James B. Hurley, "Did Paul Require Veils or the Silence of Women: A Consideration of 1 Cor. 11:2–16 and 1 Cor. 14:33b–36," p. 205.
26. Annié Jaubert, "Le Voile des Femmes (1 Cor. xi. 2–16," *New Testament Studies* 18 (1971/72):424.
27. Ibid., p. 419; This is the opposite of the thinking of Krister Stendahl, *The Bible and the Role of Women* (Philadelphia: Fortress Press, 1966), pp. 29–30.
28. See the following articles for interesting but unconvincing alternatives: W. D. Morris, "1 Corinthians xi.10," *Expository Times* 39

(1927/28), 139; E. E. Kellett, "A Note on 'Power on the Head,'" *Expository Times* 23 (1911/12):39; P. Rose, "Power on the Head," *Expository Times* 23 (1911/12):183–84.

29. The view on evil angels has often been bolstered by a reference to Jewish speculation about the sons of God in Genesis 6:2. See for a discussion of the position: James B. Hurley, "Did Paul Require Veils or the Silence of Women: A Consideration of 1 Cor. 11:2–16 and 1 Cor. 14:33b–36," p. 34; J. A. Fitzmyer, "A Feature of Qumran Angelology and the Angels of 1 Cor. 11:10, p. 54. Such Jewish speculation, however, is foreign to the New Testament where believers are freed from the power of Satan and his angels. Only obedient angels are purviewed as being at the worship of the saints (Heb. 12:22; Rev. 5:11).

30. Alexander, p. 9; Moffatt perceives Paul as reflecting on the midrash on Genesis 1:26–28 which made angels guardians of creation. James Moffatt, *The First Epistle of Paul to the Corinthians* (London: Hodder and Stoughton, 1947), p. 152; Fitzmyer sees support for angels assisting in public worship in Ps. 137:1 (138:1], *"enantion angellon psalo soi"* (LXX), and Rev. 8:3 where an angel assists prayers. Additionally, evidence from Qumran indicates the belief in angels as present at sacred gatherings. In column 7 of the *War Scroll* ceremonial cleanness was expected of those who were to go to war because of the accompaniment of angels (1 QM vii. 4–6). Also the so-called Rule of the Congregation excludes those with physical uncleanness from the congregational meetings because of the presence of angels (1 Q Sa. ii. 3–11). J. A. Fitzmyer, "A Feature of Qumran Angelology and the Angels of 1 Cor. 11:10, p. 55–56. The idea of uncleanness may also relate to the letting down of a woman's hair. An example is recounted by Jaubert concerning the sparing of On, son of Peleth, whose wife got him drunk, then took down her hair so that any coming to look for On, upon seeing her undone hair would turn aside. The display of her undone hair is related to the fact that the congregation was holy. Annié Jaubert, "Le Voile des Femmes (1 Cor. xi. 2–16," p. 426. Fitzmyer concludes from his study of Qumran material that "the unveiled head of a woman is like a bodily defect which should be excluded from such an assembly, 'because holy angels are present in their congregation.'" Fitzmyer, p. 57.

31. James B. Hurley, "Did Paul Require Veils or the Silence of Women: A Consideration of 1 Cor. 11:2–16 and 1 Cor. 14:33b–36," p. 209.

32. Ibid., pp. 209–10.

33. ꞏꞏꞏ ꞏꞏꞏꞏ ꞏꞏ ꞏꞏꞏꞏꞏꞏꞏꞏꞏꞏ ꞏꞏꞏ ꞏꞏꞏꞏ ꞏꞏꞏꞏꞏꞏꞏꞏꞏ ꞏꞏ ꞏꞏꞏꞏꞏꞏꞏꞏꞏ ꞏꞏꞏꞏꞏꞏ ꞏꞏꞏꞏꞏ ꞏꞏꞏꞏ ꞏꞏ ticulated the view that the *exousia* refers to magical power the veiled woman had against the attacks of evil spirits. O. Everling, *Die paulinische Angelologie und Damonologie* (Göttingen: Vandenhoeck and Ruprecht, 1888), p. 37; R. Reitzenstein, *Poimandres* (Leipzig: B. G. Teubner, 1904), 230, n. 1, cited from Fitzmyer, "A Feature of Qumran Angelology," 52. Though this interpretation maintains the active sense of *exousia*, it has little else in its favor. That evil angels are the a[ggeloi of the passage has already been discounted in the pertinent discussion in the text of the article. Moreover, no evidence exists that shows a veil, or

another type of covering, had such magical power in the minds of the people in the days of Paul. Another view has been proposed by Kittel. He argued that *exousia* is related to an extra-Biblical Aramaic word meaning "to have power, dominion over." G. Kittel, *"exousia" Theological Dictionary of the New Testament,* ed. Gerhard Kittel, trans. by Geoffrey W. Bromiley (Grand Rapids: Wm. B. Eerdmans Publishing Co., 1964; Hooker, "Authority on Her Head: An Examination of 1 Cor. 11:10," 413. Substantiating this view is the ancient variant reading in 1 Corinthians 11:10, where instead of *exousia* there is *kalumma.* Jerome's use of *velamen* gives additional strength. Though this view is ingenious, "Paul would surely not have made his argument depend upon a pun which was incomprehensible to his Greek readers." Hooker, 413.

34. Hooker, 413.

35. Annié Jaubert, "Le Voile des Femmes )1 Cor. xi. 2–16," 428).

36. Fitzmyer, 51.

37. F. Blass, A. Debrunner, and Robert W. Funk, *A Greek Grammar of the New Testament and Other Early Christian Literature,* p. 234, para. 449.

38. Paul Jewett, "Doctrine of Man," p. 99, cited from Letha Scanzoni and Nancy Hardesty, *All We're Meant to Be,* p. 28.

39. Ralph Alexander, "An Exegetical Presentation on 1 Corinthians 11:2–16 and 1 Timothy 2:8–15," p. 9.

40. Contra. Letha Scanzoni and Nancy Hardesty, *All We're Meant to Be,* p. 67. Paul based his view of economic relationships between man and woman upon theological considerations. He develops the equally of the male and female in essence from Genesis 1:26–28. The subordination theme is derived from Genesis 2. See my dissertation for an analysis of Genesis 2 and its headship theme, pp. 80–88.

41. Paul Jewett, *Man as Male and Female,* p. 113.

42. The word of "men" *(aner)* should not be taken as husbands but men. Certainly not just husbands are to pray in congregational worship. If he had meant husbands one would think he would have used something like *idious tous andras* (cf. 5:22). Alexander, p. 12.

43. J. W. Roberts, *Letters to Timothy* (Austin: Sweet Publishing Company, 1916), p. 21.

44. M. Dibelius and H. Conzelmann, *The Pastoral Epistles,* Hermeneia Series (Philadelphia: Fortress Press, 1972), p. 45.

45. Alexander, "An Exegetical Presentation," p. 12.

## CHAPTER EIGHT

1. There is dispute on the paragraphing. B. F. Westcott and F. Hort (*The New Testament in the Original Greek* [New York, NY: American Book Co., 1881], p. 397) concur with the *Textus Receptus* (*The New Testament According to the Received Text* [London: The British and Foreign Bible Society, 1962], p. 256) in ending the sentence with *agion,* whereas the United Bible Societies text (*The Greek New Testament,* Kurt Aland, et

al, eds. [New York; London: United Bible Societies, 1966], p. 611) and the text edited by Eberhard Nestle and Kurt Aland (*Novum Testamentum Graece* [Stuttgart: Deutsche Bibelstiftung, 1979], p. 466) begin a new paragraph with *hos*. There is awkwardness in the repetition of *ekklesias* but Jean Héring (*The First Epistle of Saint Paul to the Corinthians* [London: The Epworth Press, 1962], p. 154), Hans Conzelmann (*1 Corinthians*, Hermeneia Series [Philadelphia: Fortress Press, 1975], p. 246), and F. F. Bruce (*1 and 2 Corinthians*, New Century Bible [Greenwood, SC: The Attic Press, 1971], p. 136) avoid this problem (rightly) by taking the first usage to be a reference to the people of God and the latter to the local meeting. The mention of universal practice of the churches makes considerably more sense in reference to verses 34–35 than it does to the peace of God in verse 33a. Arguing against this is F. W. Grosheide, *Commentary on the First Epistle to the Corinthians*, New International Commentary on the New Testament [Grand Rapids: Wm. B. Eerdmans Publishing Company, 1953), p. 341; William F. Orr and James Arthur Walther, *1 Corinthians*, The Anchor Bible [Garden City, NY: Doubleday & Company, 1976), pp. 311–12.

2. F. Godet, *Commentary on the First Epistle to the Corinthians*, trans. A. Cusin [Edinburgh: T & T Clark, 1890), p. 309.

3. C. K. Barrett, *A Commentary on the First Epistle to the Corinthians*, Harper's New Testament Commentaries [New York: Harper & Row, Publishers, 1968), p. 330; Orr and Walther, p. 312; Godet, p. 308; Heinrich August Wilhelm Meyer, *Critical and Exegetical Hand-Book to the Epistles to the Corinthians* [New York: FUnk & Wagnalls, Publishers, 1884), p. 333. Bruce discounts the view that Genesis 3:16 is the source. "This is unlikely, since in MT and LXX Gen. 3:16 speaks of the woman's instinctive inclination or passionate desire (Hebrew *tᵉsuqah*, Greek *apostrophe*) towards her husband, of which he takes advantage so as to dominate her." F. F. Bruce, p. 136. However, Bruce may have the wrong understanding of the woman's desire in Genesis 3:16. The desire may not be that of passion but a desire for dominion over men. See Susah Foh, "What is the Woman's Desire," *Westminster Theological Journal* 37 (Spring 1975):377–78. Likewise, Clark disagrees with Genesis 3:16 as the basis of authority for 1 Corinthians 14:34, because it "would be the only place in the New Testament where the 'curses' of the Fall were appealed to as a basis for Christian conduct, direction, or teaching." Stephan B. Clark, *Man and Woman in Christ* [Ann Arbor, Mich.: Servant Books, 1980], p. xxx.

4. F. F. Bruce, p. 136. His position has the advantage of a previous use of Genesis 2 by Paul in 11:7–9. But in these verses the apostle gives specific information tying his argument to Genesis 2, whereas 14:34 speaks in general terms about female subordination.

5. See R. C. H. Lenski, *The Interpretation of St. Paul's First and Second Epistles to the Corinthians* [Minneapolis, Minn.: Augsburg Publishing House, 1937), p. 616. Schlatter sees the reference possibly to Miriam's punishment in her rejection of Moses' authority. Adolf Schlatter, *Paulus der Bote Jesu* [Stuttgart: Calwer Vereinsbachhandlung, 1934), p. 388.

6. Clark says, '[I]t seems unlikely that the Lord would instruct his disciples about order in assmeblies containing prophecy and tongues-speaking." Stephan Clark, *Man and Woman in Christ*, p. 188.

7. One probably should understand the woman in the Scripture at hand as married women (though the teaching almost certainly applies to the unmarried as well) since verse 35 says for them to inquire of their own husbands *(tous idious andras eperotatosan)* at home.

8. Hurley says, "His aim in v. 35 is not to prevent learning but rather to prevent a wrong exercise of authority . . . Lest the Corinthians move to the extreme of believing learning is forbidden women or because they initiated the contention in their letter, Paul says they may learn from their husbands at home. Hurley, "Did Paul Require Veils or the Silence of Women: A Consideration of 1 Cor. 11:2–16 and 1 Cor. 14:33b–36," pp. 217–18.

9. For these different arguments see Hans Conzelmann, 1 Corinthians, Hermeneia Series (Philadelphia: Fortress Press, 1975), 246; cf. Johannes Weiss, *Der erste Korintherbrief* (Göttingen: Vandenhoeck & Ruprecht, 1910), p. 342; C. K. Barrett, *A Commentary on the First Epistle to the Corinthians*, p. 332; Robert Jewett sees 1 Corinthians 14:33b-35 as being only one part of considerable redactional work done by a later Pauline school on 1 Corinthians, reflecting their concerns at that time. Robert Jewett, "The Redaction of 1 Corinthians and the Trajectory of the Pauline School," *Journal of the American Academy of Religion, Supplement* 44 (December 1978):571.

10. Frederik Willem Grosheide, *Commentary on the First Epistle to the Corinthians, The New International Commentary on the New Testament,* pp. 341–42; Clark says, "What Agabus did hardly fits into a worship service; and exegesis cannot deny that Philip's daughters prophesied, like Agabus, when no church service was in progress." Gordon Clark, "The Ordination of Women," *The Trinity Review,* no. 17 (Jan/Feb 1981);3–4; Alexander argues that "verses 2–16 appear to be an outgrowth of the previous discussion on Christian freedom and not related to the aspect of church worship." Ralph Alexander, "An Exegetical Presentation on 1 Corinthians 11:2–16 and 1 Timothy 2:8–15," p. 4.

11. Grosheide, pp. 341–42.

12. Joseph Dillow, *Speaking in Tongues: Seven Crucial Questions* (Grand Rapids: Zondervan Publishing House, 1975), p. 170. Orr also considers this probable. Orr and Walther, William F. Orr and James Arthur Walther, *1 Corinthians*, p. 313. Bruner says that verses 33b–38 concern specifically the "glosso-*lalic*" participation of women in the congregational meetings. This is in contrast to the more intelligible contributions of 1 Corinthians 11:5. Frederick Dale Bruner, *A Theology of the Holy Spirit* (Grand Rapids: William B. Eerdmans, Publisher, 1970), p. 301.

13. H. Wayne House, "Tongues and the Mystery Religions of Corinth," *Bibliotheca Sacra* 140 (April–June 1983): 134–50.

14. Jean Héring, *The First Epistle of Saint Paul to the Corinthians*, p. 154; Hurley says, "It is clear from chapter 11 that Paul did not under-

stand charismatic prayer or prophecy from women as violations of this order, as these involve no direct authority on the part of the speaker." James B. Hurley, "Did Paul Require Veils or the Silence of Women: A Consideration of 1 Cor. 11:2–16 and 1 Cor. 14:33b–36," p. 217.

15. Boyce W. Blackwelder, *Light from the Greek New Testament* (Anderson, Ind.: The Warner Press, 1958), p. 56; Lenski concurs with this interpretation and continues: "The fact that the asking of questions in the open assembly is practically equivalent to speaking publicly before the congregation . . . Paul supports the order that women should ask at home." R. C. H. Lenski, *The Interpretation of St. Paul's First and Second Epistles to the Corinthians*, p. 618; cf. also Héring, *The First Epistle of Saint Paul to the Corinthians*, p. 154; Meyer, *Critical and Exegetical Hand-Book to the Epistles to the Corinthians*, p. 334. *Laleo* is used in Hebrew 12:25 with God as subject.

16. N. J. Hommes, "Let Women Be Silent in Church," *Calvin Theological Journal* 4 (April 1969):7–16; Hurley, "Did Paul Require Veils or the Silence of Women: A Consideration of 1 Cor. 11:2–16 and 1 Cor. 14:33b–36," 217–18.

17. Cf. Stephan Clark, *Man and Woman in Christ*, pp. 185–86.

18. See Zerbst, *The Office of Women in the Church*, pp. 48–49 for a discussion on "shameful."

19. Bauer, *A Greek-English Lexicon of the New Testament and Other Early Christian Literature*, p. 464.

20. Bruce, *1 and 2 Corinthians*, pp. 135–36. Emphasis his.

21. Hurley, "Did Paul Require Veils or the Silence of Women: A Consideration of 1 Cor. 11:2–16 and 1 Cor. 14:33b–36," *Westminster Theological Journal* 35 (1973):217–18.

22. Godet, *Commentary on St. Paul's First Epistle to the Corinthians*, pp. 312–13.

23. Ibid., p. 313; Barrett, *A Commentary on the First Epistle to the Corinthians*, p. 332.

24. Groshiede, *Commentary on the First Epistle to the Corinthians*, p. 342; John Calvin said that the prohibition should probably not be enforced in well-organized churches. John Calvin, *The First Epistle of Paul the Apostle to the Corinthians*, Calvin's Commentaries (Grand Rapids: Wm. B. Eerdmans Publishing Company, 1960), pp. 306–07.

25. "The passive points back to an already valid regulation, such as we find in 1 Tim. 2;12." Weiss, *Der erste Korintherbrief*, cited from Conzelmann, *1 Corinthians*, p. 246; Walther says, "The linear jussive suggests that this is the expected condition rather than that Paul is proposing any radical regulation." Orr and Walther, *1 Corinthians*, p. 312.

26. R. Seeberg, *Über das Reden der Frauen in den apostolischen Gemeinden*, cited from Zerbst, *The Office of Woman in the Church*, p. 46.

27. Hurley, "Did Paul Require Veils or the Silence of Women: A Consideration of 1 Cor. 11:2–16 and 1 Cor. 14:33b–36," 217; Lightfoot, *The Role of Women: New Testament Perspectives*, p. 134.

28. Grosheide, *Commentary on the First Epistle to the Corinthians*, p. 342.

29. Bruce *1 and 2 Corinthians*, pp. 135–36.

30. "His aim in v 35 is not to prevent learning but rather to prevent a wrong exercise of authority. It helps the modern reader to understand that men and women were separated in the synagogues. It is very likely that the pattern was followed by the new church at Corinth. The women were therefore unable to reach their husbands to talk with them during the service itself, to say nothing of the disturbance which this talking might have caused. Paul's instructions are thus geared to the situation which existed. They prevent a wrong use of authority but guard the instruction of the women, with which Paul was vitally concerned. Hurley, pp. 217–18; likewise Zerbst, p. 48.

31. Conzelmann, *1 and 2 Corinthians*, p. 246; Lenski, *The Interpretation of St. Paul's First and Second Epistles to the Corinthians*, p. 618.

32. Godet, *Commentary on St. Paul's First Epistle to the Corinthians*, p. 313.

33. Hurley, "Did Paul Require Veils or the Silence of Women: A Consideration of 1 Cor. 11:2–16 and 1 Cor. 14:33b–36," 217.

34. Clark, *Men and Women in Christ*, p. 192.

35. Philip Payne, "Libertarian Women in Ephesus: A Response to Douglas J. Moo's Article, '1 Timothy 2:11–15: Meaning and Significance,'"*Trinity Journal* 2 (1981):185–97; Aída Besançon Spencer, "Eve at Ephesus," *Journal of the Evangelical Theological Society* 17 (Fall 1974):215–22; Scanzoni and Hardesty, *All We're Meant to Be*, pp. 70–71.

36. Ibid., p. 174; Hommes argues that teaching should be understood as referring to dialogue, not monologue. N. J. Hommes, "Let Women Be Silent in Church," *Calvin Theological Journal* 4 (April 1969):7–16.

37. Payne, "Libertarian Women in Ephesus," p. 175.

38. Hommes, pp. 18–20.

39. Payne, "Libertarian Women in Ephesus," pp. 175–177.

40. Spencer, "Eve at Ephesus," p. 216.

41. Ibid.

42. Ibid.

43. Moo, "1 Timothy 2:11–15: Meaning and Significance," p. 200.

44. See Clark, *Man and Woman in Christ*, p. 200.

45. Ibid., pp. 196–197.

46. Theodore Jungkuntz, "The Question of the Ordination of Women," *The Cresset*, 42 (December 1978):18.

47. Carroll D. Osburn, ' in Reference to Women in 1 Timothy 2.12," *New Testament Studies* 30 (January 1984):143–57.

49. Bauer, *A Greek-English Lexicon of the New Testament and Other Early Christian Literature*, p. 151; H. E. Dana and Julius R. Mantey, *A Manual Grammar of the Greek New Testament* (New York: Macmillan, 1927), p. 243; Maximilian Zerwick, *Biblical Greek* (Rome: Pontifical Biblical Press, 1963)x, 473.

50. For example, 1 Timothy 3:13; 4:5, 8, 16;5:4, 11, 15.

51. Moo, "The Interpretation of 1 Timothy 2:11–15," pp. 215–21.
52. Dibelius and Conzelmann, *The Pastoral Epistles, Hermeneia Series,*
p. 47.
53. Alexander, "An Exegetical Presentation on 1 Corinthians 11:2–16
and 1 Timothy 2:8–15," p. 13.
54. See my dissertation for an analysis of Genesis 3:16b, pp. 165–71;
also see Susan Foh, "What is the Woman's Desire?" *Westminster Theological Journal* 37 (Spring 1975):380–81.
55. Phyllis Trible, "Eve and Adam: Genesis 2–3 Reread," *Andover Newton Quarterly* 13 (1973):251.

# CHAPTER NINE

1. In a letter from Pliny to Trajan at the beginning of the second century
concerning the Christians at Pontus, he writes: "I have judged it necessary to obtain information by torture from two serving women *(ancillae)* called by them 'deaconesses' *(ministrae),*" the latter term being
probably a translation of diakonos". Jean Daniélou, *The Ministry of
Women in the Early Church,* trans. Glyn Simon (Leighton Buzzard: The
Faith Press, 1961), p. 15.
2. Leonard, p. 316.
3. Letha Scanzoni and Nancy Hardesty, *All We're Meant to Be* (Waco,
Tx.: Word Books, 1974), p. 62.
4. John Murray, *The Epistle to the Romans, The New International
Commentary on the New Testament,* 2 vols. (Grand Rapids: Wm B.
Eerdmans Publishing Co., 1965),2:226.
5. Walter Bauer, *A Greek-English Lexicon of the New Testament and
Other Early Christian Literature,* trans. William F. Arndt and F. Wilbur
Gingrich (Chicago: The University of Chicago Press, 1957), p. 726.
6. James Hope Moulton and George Milligan, *The Vocabulary of the
Greek Testament* (Grand Rapids: Wm. B. Eerdmans Publishing Company, 1930), p. 551.
7. Murray, p. 227, f.n.
8. Evelyn and Frank Stagg, *Woman in the World of Jesus* (Philadelphia:
The Westminster Press, 1978), p. 202.
9. Colin Brown, ed., "Woman," *The New International Dictionary of
New Testament Theology,* vol. 3 (Grand Rapids: Zondervan Publishing
House, 1978), p. 1065.
10. M. Dibelius and H. Conzelmann, *The Pastoral Epistles,* Hermeneia
SEries (Philadelphia: Fortress Press, 1972), p. 58.
11. Henry Alford, *The Greek Testament,* vol. 3: *Galatians-Philemon*
(Chicago: Moody Press, 1958 reprint), p. 327.

# Select Bibliography

Stephen Clark. *Men and Women in Christ* (Ann Arbor, Mich.: Servant Books, 1980).

Jean Danielou, translated by Glyn Simon. *The Ministry of Women in the Early Church* (Leighton Buzzard: Faith Press, 1961).

James B. Hurley. *Man and Woman in Biblical Perspective* (Grand Rapids, Mich.: Zondervan Publishing House, 1981).

Paul Jewett. *Man as Male and Female* (Grand Rapids, Mich.: Wm. B. Eerdmans Publishing Co., 1975).

George W. Knight III. *The Role Relationship of Men and Women* (Chicago, Ill.: Moody Press, 1985).

Alvera Mickelson, ed. *Women, Authority and the Bible* (Downers Grove, Ill.: InterVarsity Press, 1986).

Virginia Mollenkott. *Women, Men, and the Bible* (Nashville, Tenn.: Abingdon Press, 1977).

Charles Ryrie. *The Role of Women in the Bible* (Chicago, Ill.: Moody Press, 1968).

Letha Scanzoni and Nancy Herdesty. *All We're Meant to Be* (Waco, Tex.: Word Books, 1974).

Gilbert Silezikian. *Beyond Sex Roles* (Grand Rapids, Mich.: Baker Book House, 1986).

Kirster Stendahl, translated by Emilie T. Sander. *The Bible and the Role of Women* (Philadelphia, Penn.: Fortress Press, 1966).

Fritz Zerbst. *The Office of Woman in the Church* (St. Louis, Mo.: Concordia Publishing House, 1955).

# Scripture Index